Advance Praise for
Is God a Vegetarian?

"A gentle spirit suffuses *Is God a Vegetarian?*, appropriately matching its explicitly Christian vegetarian witness. Guided by a theological vision of the peaceable kingdom initiated by Christ, Richard Alan Young refuses to shame us with moralisms about animal rights; instead, he invites us to consider the whole of the Christian message of repentance, justice, and concern for all of God's creatures as it might lead us to vegetarianism.

"The biblical case Young makes is strengthened by his ready admission that Jesus and his first disciples likely ate meat, for it marks Young's present witness to vegetarianism as part of the ongoing story of the church as it responds to God's call in various ages. The clear and simple language of the book masks its theological sophistication. Young is aware of and deftly uses important current theological and philosophical trends such as narrative theology, virtue ethics, and a revitalized ecclesiology. Like those by Andrew Linzey, Young's book shows us how vegetarianism can be defended without sacrificing theological integrity or othodoxy. The thoughtful Christian cannot leave *Is God a Vegetarian?* without feeling deeply challenged in her daily habits of life and mind."

— CHARLES PINCHES, Professor of Theology, University of Scranton
Co-author of *Good News for Animals?*

"Richard Alan Young has combined a bold thesis—that a morally responsible Christianity demands serious consideration of vegetarianism as a way of honoring creation in all its richness—with a nuanced reading of the Bible and the tradition that respects the complexity of the issues involved. Plus he offers recipes! He may not change your way of eating, but he will certainly change your way of thinking about what you are eating."

— LUKE TIMOTHY JOHNSON, Candler School of Theology,
Emory University

"Hurray for Richard Alan Young! ... of vegetarianism for those of us Christ ... guide to faith and morals. I plan to w ... the Christmas tree for my mom, dad, .

— GARY L. COMSTOCK, Co-ordinator, Bio-ethics ...
Iowa State University

Is God a Vegetarian?

Christianity, Vegetarianism, and Animal Rights

RICHARD ALAN YOUNG

With a Foreword by
Carol J. Adams

OPEN COURT
Chicago and La Salle, Illinois

To order books from Open Court, call toll-free 1-800-815-2280.

Cover painting reproduced by permission of the Art Institute of Chicago: André Derain, French, 1880–1854. *The Last Supper,* oil on canvas, 1911, 226.7 × 288.3 cm. Gift of Mrs. Frank R. Lillie, 1946.339, photograph © 1996 The Art Institute of Chicago. All Rights Reserved.

Library of Congress Cataloging-in-Publication Data

Young, Richard A., 1944–
    Is God a vegetarian? : Christianity, vegetarianism, and animal rights / Richard Alan Young : with a foreword by Carol J. Adams.
        p.   cm.
    Includes bibliographical references (p.   ) and indexes.
    ISBN 0-8126-9393-0 (paperback)
    1. Vegetarianism—Religious aspects—Christianity.   2. Animal rights—Religious aspects—Christianity.   3. Vegetarianism—Biblical teaching.   4. Animal welfare—Biblical teaching   5. Vegetarian cookery.   I. Title.
BT749.Y68   1999
241'.693—dc21   98-27827
                                                                         CIP

Contents

Foreword by Carol J. Adams   vii

Preface   xi

Introduction   xv

1. Was Jesus a Vegetarian?   1

2. Would a Veggie Garfield Be a Happy Cat?   15

3. Was God the First Tanner?   28

4. Was Noah's Ark an Early Food Factory?   41

5. Didn't God Permit Us to Eat Meat?   53

6. Isn't Passover Lamb the Main Entrée?   65

7. Was Jesus Kosher?   77

8. Didn't John the Baptist Snack on Locusts?   90

9. Doesn't God Care about Our Health?   102

10. Didn't Paul Condemn Vegetarianism as Heresy?   115

11. Is Christian Vegetarianism Only for Desert Monks?   127

12. Will There Be Slaughterhouses in Heaven?   140

13. What Then Shall We Eat?   153

Epilogue: Going Vegetarian   167

Further Reading   178

General Index   181

Recipe Index   187

Foreword

"Lord, have we ever seen you suffer as a veal calf? Or imprisoned as a laying hen? Or slaughtered as a fish, or a cow, or a pig?"

"Truly I tell you, just as you did it not to one of the least of these, you did not do it to me."

This version of the famous Matthew 25 passage is not in my Bible, nor is it in yours. Yet after reading Richard Alan Young's thoughtful and important book, I believe that the animals who are consumed as food qualify as "one of the least of these."

It is the success of this book that it does not argue, it compels. He does not insist "We must do it this way because that is how it was done in the Bible." Instead he suggests "As Christians we must consider the current situation of animals, and the environment, and our health; decisions in these areas of our lives are not divorced from our understanding of what it means to be Christian." Faithful living in community transcends human bonding; it requires faithful action that works to break the bonds that injure our fellow creatures—bonds of our own design.

Richard Young has settled for no simple task. He does not turn to the Bible to vindicate his own view. We learn how both vegetarians and meat eaters err by approaching the Scriptures for "sound bites" for their dietary choices. Instead, Young approaches the Scriptures with a sense of God's ongoing revelation in human history, and asks of any event or statement: "Is this true for us now?" Young's comprehensive, but accessible, review of contentious passages in the Bible and the early church describes what was appropriate then and asks "what is appropriate now?" He approaches the texts he examines as he would have us relate to animals—with sensitivity and care.

Our spirituality could be said to represent our journey in living authentic lives. We read the Bible to give us guidance for that journey. It maps our direction. Young helps unravel the many passages that can befuddle us as we try to decide what does such authentic living require of us today?

From Genesis 1:26, in which God appears to grant dominion to humankind, a deeply held view predominates among some of the faithful that animals are ours to use. Indeed, I often joke that even atheists believe they have a God-given right to eat animals. This is only one of many passages that Young illuminates. His goal is not to make it conform to his viewpoint, but to provide the context so that we can interact with that passage with intelligence and with a consciousness that our world today is not the same as the world we find in the pages of the Bible.

As long as we believe that God granted dominion, that Jesus ate meat, that Paul rejected vegetarianism, *and that therefore we are entitled to eat meat,* we misrepresent our own ethical choices as well as what the Bible is telling us. It is much simpler to believe that "someone, but not me, is responsible for these animals' death. Because I am not responsible, I don't have to examine what I am doing." Young says, "not so fast." He rejects as well some vegetarians' zeal to find the historical vegetarian Jesus. To both sides, he insists, our quest must be to acquire the ability to discern what justice requires of us today.

A friend who teaches pastoral care defines spirituality as answering the question "to what do I commit my life?" Each daily choice becomes in the aggregate an ethical commitment. The most frequent relationship the majority of Christians have with the other animals is with dead animals whom they eat, for breakfast or lunch or dinner. Young helps us see exactly how this choice, either unexamined, or strongly defended, becomes in the aggregate a commitment to a system that costs animals, our health, and the environment dearly. When I decided to stop eating animals and animal products, I was saying, "I will not commit my life, unexamined meal by unexamined meal, to a system of injustice and violence."

One of the few feminine images of divinity presented in the New Testament draws on an image from the world of animals: "How often have I desired to gather your children together as a hen gathers her brood under her wings, and you were not willing!" (Luke 13:34). Jesus' metaphor of the hen gathering her chicks is not a scene found on any factory farm today.

We need not require an extensive system of suffering, imprisonment, and slaughtering for our sustenance. Removing animals from our diet enables us to greet Creation in a new way. Grace-filled moments await everyone who brings grace into their dinners, vegetarian meal by vegetarian meal.

In the Bible, vegetarianism is situated in the beginning and in the fulfillment of time. Young beckons us to situate vegetarianism in the present-time. What we forfeit—comfortable misreadings and traditional tastes—pale before what we gain.

"Lord, have we ever seen you suffer as a veal calf? Or imprisoned as a laying hen? Or slaughtered as a fish, or a cow, or a pig?"

"Truly I tell you, just as you did it to one of the least of these who are members of my family, you did it to me."

CAROL J. ADAMS

Preface

My wife and I have been vegetarians for about ten years. Our journey has been gradual. For about fifteen years before becoming vegetarians we were removing things from our diet we felt were not healthy, such as butter, sugar, fatty meats, and sausage. We were content at that stage with replacing butter with vegetable oils, white sugar with brown sugar (and then honey), and fatty meats with lean cuts.

When we learned about foodborne diseases in meat as well as the antibiotics and hormones injected into livestock, we slowly began eliminating red meat from our diet, being satisfied at that time with fish, chicken, eggs, and milk. Then we found out about salmonella poisoning in eggs, about the way chickens are raised in factory farms, and about putrefaction in fish. In 1992 I heard a lecture by Dr. John McDougall at a health conference in which he argued that milk was not necessary for one's health. Letting go of milk was a struggle, but now we are total vegetarians, partaking only of vegetables, grains, fruits, legumes, and nuts.

Our trek was guided mostly by health reasons and only partially by ethical reasons. The religious aspect was not a consideration at all. However, being contemplative religious people, we began observing the way church people ate, mulling over what the Scriptures had to say, and asking questions about diet and spirituality. We have come to realize that a vegetarian diet is part of a whole way of being, a way of being that is physically, ethically, environmentally, and spiritually healthy for ourselves, others, and the entire planet. We have also discovered that the religious and spiritual aspects of vegetarianism are of fundamental importance in that they tie the other threads together and give our diet meaning and significance in our lives.

The title of the book is designed to lead us into the discussion. The title, of course, is not intended literally, since Christians do not perceive of God as eating food. Nor is it intended as a projection of what we want God to be like; that is, to make God in our image. A Christian concept of God must be shaped by the Christian Scriptures.

Rather the title is a questioning metaphor that probes into the very being of God. What is God like? Is not the God of the Bible a God of love, justice, and peace, who would never kill to satisfy selfish desires, who sides with the oppressed, and who would like us to live at peace without killing and war? If this is how we understand and experience God, then what metaphor best expresses that in today's context? It would be analogous to the question, Is God a mighty fortress? How did Luther (and David before him) come to understand God as a fortress? Was it not by experiencing God as a shield against all foes? The questions we must ask are, How do we experience God today? and What symbol or model (as Sallie McFague would say) meaningfully expresses our experiences in light of Scripture and in light of our contemporary social location? We should note that vegetarianism is more than diet. It is an orientation to life that encompasses love, justice, peace, and wholeness. As with all analogies, there will be similarities and differences.

Throughout the book you will find parenthetical notation rather than footnotes or endnotes. If you encounter an abbreviated entry, such as an author's name in the text and a page number after the quotation, it means the reference is cited in full earlier in the chapter or in the "Further Reading" list at the end of the book.

At the end of each chapter you will find a couple of recipes. These represent some of our favorites. The recipes are made without animal products and visible oils. Ingredients not normally found at regular stores (such as soy milk, millet, yeast flakes, and carob powder) are readily available at natural food stores.

I would like to personally thank those who helped and encouraged me on this project over the past five years, among whom are Andrew Linzey, Kerri Mommer, Luke Timothy Johnson, Timothy Staveteig, Ferrell Wheeler, Barry Zalph, Abbot Bernard Johnson, Ellis Potter, Bernell Baldwin, Douglas Bennett, Al and Donna Patt, Tisa Houck, and above all, my wife, Laura, a professional reference librarian, who helped track down many needed sources, edited numerous draft copies, and helped me reason through many knotty problems. While many have given help, I take full responsibility for the final form of the discussions.

Introduction

Vegetarianism is no longer considered a fad, something practiced only by health fanatics or rebels against the establishment. According to a 1991 Gallup Poll conducted for the National Restaurant Association, between 20 and 30 percent of the American population is interested in eating vegetarian food. According to a 1994 Roper Poll conducted for the Vegetarian Resource Group, between .3 percent and 1 percent of the population never eats meat. This means that there are between one-half and two million actual vegetarians in this country (*Vegetarian Journal*, July/August 1994). Most people abstain from meat for health or ethical reasons.

A vegetarian is one who abstains from eating animal flesh. This includes beef, pork, mutton, fish, and poultry. The term "vegetarian" dates back to the early 1840s. Before that time those who abstained from animal flesh were called Pythagoreans, flesh-abstainers, or non–meat eaters. The word sometimes gives the impression that only vegetables are eaten. Vegetarians, however, partake of a wide variety of foods, such as grains, vegetables, legumes, fruits, berries, seeds, nuts, dairy products, eggs, and honey.

Vegetarians are classified by what they eat: **ovovegetarians** will eat eggs; **lactovegetarians** will eat dairy products; **ovo-lactovegetarians** will eat both eggs and dairy products; **total vegetarians** exclude all animal products from their diet, such as eggs, dairy products, honey, gelatin, and Worcestershire sauce; **vegans** not only exclude all animal products from their diet but also avoid using any product derived from animals, such as leather, furs, silk, wool, feathers, and tallow-based soaps.

The only other time in the history of Western culture when vegetarianism made inroads into mainline society was in ancient Greece. It was advocated by some of the leading Greek writers, such as Pythagoras, Plutarch, Plotinus, and Porphyry. They were motivated by their vision of a primeval golden age where there was perfect peace and harmony.

Some suggest that vegetarianism's death knell in the West was due to the influence of the Aristotelian hierarchical system where animals exist for the sake of humanity and the Judeo-Christian tradition where God permits killing animals for food. The dualism of Descartes and the ascendancy of our affluent, materialistic society seemingly put the final touches on the West's meat-eating tradition.

The environmental movement of the 1970s, however, gave rebirth to vegetarianism. Modern vegetarianism has grown from a radical counterculture fad into a mainstream practice of Western society. Increasing numbers of people are realizing the environmental, ethical, and health implications of a meatless diet. Nevertheless, there is a large segment of the population that remains rather fixed in its meat-eating tradition. Among this number are most Bible-believing Christians, some of whom are even antagonistic toward vegetarianism. Anyone who has ever attended a church dinner is well aware that the typical fare is anything but vegetarian.

Biblical Christianity and vegetarianism seem worlds apart. After all, did not God give humans dominion over the animals to use them as they wish (Gen 1:28)? Did not God permit humans to eat the flesh of animals after the flood (Gen 9:3)? Did not God command sacrifices to be offered and allow the people to eat the meat? For many Christians the decisive point regarding the issue of vegetarianism is that Jesus not only ate fish (Luke 24:42–43) but also multiplied the loaves and fish so all could eat. To top it off, Paul fully endorses the eating of meat and condemns those who advocate vegetarianism (1 Tim 4:1–3). It would appear that the Bible unquestionably sanctions a meat-eating diet.

Why then does the author of Genesis have God prescribing a vegetarian diet to Adam and Eve in the garden (Gen 1:29)? Why do the apocalyptic visions of Isaiah and John depict the restoration of peace and harmony in creation along with an implied vegetarian diet? According to the biblical narrative, our roots and destiny are grounded in vegetarianism. Since the biblical story is bracketed on both ends with visions of creation peace, it seems incongruous for Christians to be indifferent toward vegetarianism. Does meat eating represent a departure from the hope of creation harmony that God placed in the hearts of the biblical writers?

But how can vegetarianism be a Christian concern when God permits, Jesus practices, and Paul sanctions meat eating? There is no question that there are two conflicting dietary motifs in Scripture. How should we proceed? I would like to suggest that we must respect both sets of voices and let them be heard. But they must be heard within their own social location, something not often done.

Part of the problem of not listening is that when there are conflicting voices in Scripture on what the church deems peripheral issues we tend to let our own social location rule our selection of texts and either ignore, explain away, or harmonize the contrary texts. That is, we let the norms of culture become norms of the church. We live in a materialistic culture that is still under the spell of Aristotle's hierarchical system. This hierarchical system passed into Christian theology through Thomas Aquinas and is seen in such writers as John Calvin, who says that the universe was made especially for human use and enjoyment (*Institutes of the Christian Religion* 1.16.6). This enlightens us about the continuing need to critique our own presuppositions, traditions, and social context so that we can listen with an open ear to what Scripture has to say.

My approach is to listen to the entire story rather than appealing to selected prooftexts. The primary questions I will be asking are, Where is the story going? and How does the story shape our lives? The Bible is primarily narrative; that is, it tells a story about a people struggling with their identity and with how to relate to God and others. It tells of a journey over some rather rough terrain, with some pilgrims bogging down along the way, others taking detours with killing, wars, and the like. In other words, there are many stories within the story. However, arising out of the diversity is a general orientation to guide pilgrims on their travels. It is primarily through this larger story that Christians shape their perceptions of God, self, and the world.

The story begins with creation and the garden of Eden, continues with the exodus, wilderness wanderings, conquest of Canaan, divided kingdom, exile and return, the incarnation, Christ's resurrection victory over sin and death, and consummates with the peaceable kingdom. It is a story of "hope for the hopeless," as Jürgen Moltmann calls it (*The Experiment Hope*, Fortress, 1975, p. 57); it is a story in which we are invited to enter and participate. As we place our story within God's story we find a new way of seeing the world and a new way of living. Our lives will begin to reflect the God who brought us into being and who is leading us toward peaceful coexistence with the entire creation community.

The book could be viewed as an experiment in a narrative approach to the text that focuses around a single cluster of issues—vegetarianism and attitudes toward animals. These issues raise a myriad of ethical problems. Is it categorically wrong to kill animals for food? If so, then most people would be guilty of immorality every time they sit down for a meal. But then what about the morality of animal factories and abusive methods of raising veal calves, pigs, and chickens? Are such practices categorically wrong, and if so, what makes them wrong? What makes anything right or wrong? Do we have absolute rules that stand above any particular situation? Then what about occasionally eating a humanely raised chicken? Would that be wrong? What about economic practices that feed the rich with meat raised in Third World countries where the people hardly have resources to feed themselves? What about the sacredness of life and unnecessarily hurting sentient creatures? When we begin talking about the ethics of diet, we are immediately struck with an array of problems. How are we as followers of Christ to work through these questions and live ethically in this present age?

There are three primary ways people think about ethics. First, deontological (rule-based) ethics emphasizes duty to a law or principle regardless of its outcome. Second, teleological (outcome-based) ethics contends that the consequence of an act determines whether it is right or wrong. Third, virtue ethics holds that one's character or disposition determines morality. Virtues and vices issue in noble or ignoble actions which cannot be reduced to rules that exist prior to a situation. Virtue ethics asks the question, What am I to be? whereas the first two ways of doing ethics ask the question, What am I to do?

A narrative approach to the text lends itself to virtue ethics. Narrative functions in two ways. First, it functions as a guideline for the journey. Guidelines are flexible orienters which are not held over us as absolute law. As we work through the biblical story, we will find directional markers emerging from the text that serve as pointers for the journey, such as peace, community, resurrection, compassion, renewal, and the imitation of God. Second, as we enter and participate in the direction of the narrative, we find that our inner character and dispositions become shaped by the story. A virtue approach to ethics reflects the ethics of Jesus, who focuses on inner dispositions, and the New Covenant (Jer 31:33–34; Heb 8:8–12), in which God's laws are written on the heart instead of on stone. Virtues are always formed and expressed within a community in light of the orientation of one's story. It is incumbent then to know what is happening in our community and where our story is going.

When working with narrative, one must be cautious about reducing the end of the story to abstract and universally binding rules. Doing this belies the very nature of narrative. A narrative bids us to enter and participate. As we enter the story, we do not see universal principles. What we see is a story of a people and their loving and merciful God on a journey together. To maintain the integrity of the narrative, we must identify with it rather than reduce it to something other than what it is. That is, we cannot reduce narrative to rational abstract rules that exist apart from the story without destroying the power of the story to transform character. Virtues are primary, since rules do not work too well if virtues are lacking.

Some argue for vegetarianism as an absolute and universal ethical norm. However, in doing so one encounters problems with Scripture, the Christian tradition, and real life situations. It would presume an act is either right or wrong regardless of the situation, one's attitude, or how it turns out. But how can one contend for vegetarianism in this manner? Would it be ethically wrong for a person who may otherwise die of starvation in a famine-ridden country to kill a chicken for food? Would it be ethically wrong for isolated Eskimos who cannot gather enough fruits and vegetables to sustain life to kill fish, seals, and caribou for food? Would it not be better to appeal to the virtues of love, compassion, temperance, and justice for working out what to eat in certain situations?

Enlightened Christianity avoids the immature legalism that would demand vegetarianism and replaces it with a mature faith that allows freedom to participate in God's narrative and to grow in conformity to the image of God by nurturing virtues. The genius of Christianity is that it is beyond law (as a legalistic observance) but not without law (as an inward disposition of a regenerate heart informed by the Word and Spirit).

We should also note theological ethics will differ a bit from moral philosophy in that it is grounded in God and God's relation to the world. Narrative ethics in particular presumes that one identifies in faith with a particular story, a story that contains such elements as creation, incarnation, and the resurrection. This makes it difficult to impose the conclusions we reach on those who do not accept the story. However, this does not mean that the Christian community cannot make the kingdom visible and protest against the evils in society as they participate in God's narrative.

1

Was Jesus a Vegetarian?

*And when he had said this, he showed them his hands and his feet.
While in their joy they were disbelieving and still wondering, he said
to them, "Have you anything here to eat?" They gave him a piece of
broiled fish, and he took it and ate in their presence.* (Luke 24:40–43)

*The ethics of reverence for life is the ethics of Jesus, philosophically
expressed, made cosmic in scope, and conceived as intellectually
necessary.* (Albert Schweitzer, *Pilgrimage to Humanity*, Philosophical
Library, 1961, p. 87)

Several years ago a friend confronted me with the question, "How
can a Christian argue for vegetarianism when Jesus ate fish and
the Passover lamb?" The question is quite common. Christians are
Christian because they follow Jesus. If Jesus ate meat, then meat
eating must be acceptable for his followers. Moreover, Jesus is
considered to be the model of proper conduct. To renounce meat
eating as morally wrong would be to incriminate Jesus and
demolish one of the last paragons of moral excellence we have.

Does the Bible Say Jesus Ate Meat?

Before exploring my friend's question, we need to examine what the Bible says about Jesus' eating habits. The only passage in Scripture that clearly states that Jesus ate meat is the post-resurrection appearance recorded in Luke 24:40–43 (quoted above). Scholars claim that this passage is most likely a later addition to the oral tradition designed to refute Docetic teachings that Jesus was a mere apparition. Even if this were the case, the passage would still point to Jesus' actual dietary habits, for we would not expect later traditions to radically depart from the *kinds* of things Jesus actually said and did. If Jesus was a staunch vegetarian, this episode would never have passed into the tradition as it now stands, simply because many who had been with Jesus and knew what he ate were still alive and were part of the tradition-forming community. The passage therefore supports the idea that Jesus probably ate fish.

What about Jesus' eating the Passover lamb? This is a rather debatable topic. First, the Bible does not state that Jesus ate the Passover lamb. Second, it is not certain that the last supper was the Passover meal. Third, even if it was the Passover meal, there is the possibility suggested by New Testament scholar Joachim Jeremias that Jesus abstained from eating. The basic problem is that the Synoptic Gospels imply that the last supper was the Passover meal (Matt 26:17–19; Mark 14:12–16; Luke 22:7–16), whereas John implies that it was a farewell meal before the Passover feast was celebrated (John 13:1, 29, 18:28). There have been numerous theories advanced to reconcile the accounts, but for our purposes the question must remain open.

But doesn't the Bible say that "Jesus sat at meat in the house" (Matt 9:10)? Yes, it does if you have a King James Version. However, the word "meat" in the King James Version is usually the translation for various Greek words that simply mean "food." On occasion these words may carry specific connotations, such as in John 21:5 where it probably refers to a fish relish served along with bread. Thus the word "meat" in the King James Version cannot be used to show what kind of food Jesus ate.

It is very likely that Jesus partook of the normal foods of his culture (including fish and wine). In Matthew 11:18–19 Jesus remarks, "John came neither eating nor drinking, and they say, 'He has a demon'; the Son of Man came eating and drinking, and they say, 'Look, a glutton and a drunkard, a friend of tax collectors and sinners!'" The passage contrasts John the Baptist's asceticism with Jesus' partaking of the normal fare. The diet of common people was frugal compared to our diet but probably included red meat on special occasions. Fish, however, was regularly eaten by ordinary people (especially near the Sea of Galilee) and may have been considered a necessary supplement to the diet. One would expect that Jesus, being from Galilee, ate fish.

There doesn't seem to be any good reason to reject the biblical traditions about Jesus eating fish. The traditions have Jesus not only eating fish (Luke 24:43) but also multiplying fish and loaves for the multitudes (Matt 14:13–21, 15:32–39), working miracles to help his disciples catch large quantities of fish (Luke 5:4–6; John 21:6–8), and even cooking a meal of fish over an open fire for his disciples (John 21:9–13).

Fishing for a Vegetarian Jesus

Now we're in a pickle. Jesus ate meat. By the way, meat is the flesh of any animal, including fish. If Jesus ate meat, then we are back on square one—Jesus' eating habits clash with the contemporary ethical protest against eating meat. An easy way out is to reject what the Bible implies and reconstruct a vegetarian Jesus. This is nothing new. Reconstructions that present a vegetarian Jesus, such as the *Gospel of the Ebionites,* circulated in Syria in the second and third centuries. The modern quest for the historical Jesus, which became somewhat of a fad during the eighteenth and nineteenth centuries, turned out a variety of reconstructions, some of which also present a vegetarian Jesus. However, in 1906 with the publication of *The Quest for the Historical Jesus,* Albert Schweitzer called the entire escapade into question. Schweitzer demonstrated that the Jesuses being created were merely projections of what the authors felt to be the "proper" Jesus for their particular age.

But the quest was never entirely laid to rest. It has changed its face several times since Schweitzer, but it still continues. And properly used, it does have its place. However, the quest is often driven by the assumption that the only valid model for Christian life is the historical Jesus. Later developments in the New Testament and church history are viewed as deviations from true Christianity—true Christianity being defined by what Jesus said and did. In academic circles the quest has become rather sophisticated with source, form, and redaction criticism. The quest also continues on the popular level with the New Age Jesus of the *Aquarian Gospel* and the vegetarian Jesus of *The Gospel of the Holy Twelve.* The problem with any attempted reconstruction, whether scholarly or popular, is that subjective elements undermine its supposed objectivity and authority. Consciously or unconsciously, the attempts seek to fit Jesus into a certain mold.

What about recent books that set forth a vegetarian Jesus? Aren't they backed by sound research? Well, let's take a look at them. First there is Charles Vaclavik, a Quaker medical doctor, who wrote *The Vegetarianism of Jesus Christ: The Pacifism, Communalism, and Vegetarianism of Primitive Christianity.* Vaclavik bases his reconstruction mostly on church fathers and ancient historians. Like many writers of this genre, he argues that the Essenes (the inhabitants of the Dead Sea community at Qumran) were vegetarian, that Jesus was an Essene, that the earliest Christian community continued Jesus' vegetarianism, that meat eating soon crept into the church, and that the New Testament was corrupted by later editors to purge "original" vegetarian statements. This purging was supposedly done to appease meat-eating pagans who were becoming Christians.

Another approach is represented by Upton Clary Ewing, author of *The Essene Christ* and *The Prophet of the Dead Sea Scrolls.* Ewing merges Albert Schweitzer's concept of reverence for life with Essene materials from the Dead Sea Scrolls to reconstruct a more humane Jesus, one who would be the exemplar of the highest and most noble ethic. Included in *The Essene Christ* is a reconstructed gospel in which Ewing purges all violence to animals and nature. For example, the five thousand are fed with bread, not bread and fish. Also the fig tree is blessed, not cursed. Ewing's reconstructed gospel demonstrates how easily such "gospels" can be written and that there is a continuing desire to create a Jesus more to one's liking. Although Ewing clearly states that his "gospel" was his own creation, it testifies to a growing genre of modern-day apocryphal and pseudepigraphal writings whose authors are not as honest as Ewing.

A rather esoteric approach is taken by Edmond Szekely (d. 1980). Szekely advocated vegetarianism and what he calls "biogenic living." Biogenic living could be defined as natural healing and health through eating whole, natural raw foods, hydrotherapy, breathing clean air, and bathing in sunshine. His writings differ from Vaclavik and Ewing in that they present a form of gnostic Christianity. The major themes, however, are still there—the Essenes were vegetarian and Jesus was an Essene. Proof that Jesus was vegetarian is based on *The Essene Gospel of Peace*, which Szekely claims to have translated from an ancient text he supposedly discovered in the 1920s. Szekely alleges that this ancient gospel text is authentic and that the canonical gospels are forgeries. However, no one besides Szekely has ever seen the manuscript. This and other reasons prompt scholars to conclude that *The Essene Gospel of Peace* is a disreputable forgery.

A similar tactic was taken by Gideon Jasper Ouseley (1835–1906). Ouseley served as an Anglican clergyman for about ten years before leaving the church. He was a vegetarian and had strong interests in the occult, theosophy, animal welfare, and antivivisectionism. It appears that Ouseley created *The Gospel of the Holy Twelve* in support of animal welfare and vegetarianism. Every reference in the canonical gospels to meat eating has been altered. For example, the father of the prodigal son says, "Bring hither the best ripe fruits and the bread and the oil and the wine" instead of "Get the fattened calf and kill it" (Luke 15:23). And Jesus fed the multitude with six loaves and seven clusters of grapes rather than bread and fish. *The Gospel of the Holy Twelve* also depicts Jesus as giving the "Twelve Commandments" to replace the Ten Commandments given by Moses. The third commandment forbids the eating of flesh. Jesus then remarks, "Verily

I say unto you, they who believe and obey this law [the twelve commandments] shall be saved, and they who know and obey it not, shall be lost." Since the peculiar readings lack manuscript support and are sometimes anachronistic, scholars conclude that it too is a forgery (cf. Per Beskow, *Strange Tales about Jesus,* Fortress, 1983).

A more clever approach is taken by Carl Anders Skriver (1903–1983). Skriver was born in Germany, became a vegetarian early in life, and studied philosophy, theology, and Eastern religions at various German universities. For twenty-five years he served as a Lutheran minister. Skriver was active in several vegetarian societies and in 1952 even founded his own society, the Order of the Nazoreans. His book *The Forgotten Beginnings of Creation and Christianity* depicts Jesus as a vegetarian who condemns animal sacrifices. Skriver combines ancient gnostic teachings about two creations with source criticism. The first creation (Gen 2:4–3:24) is spiritual and is the work of Yahweh. When evil invaded this pristine creation, humans were expelled from the spiritual realm and clothed with garments of flesh (the fall). The second creation (Gen 1:1–2:3) is material and is the work of Elohim (the pantheon of gods or demiurges). Elohim, who also fell, took control of the earth, and declared that flesh eating was permissible (Gen 9:3). Flesh eating then was not the idea of the good God Yahweh, but the bad God Elohim. Skriver contends that New Testament writers falsely portrayed Jesus in light of their meat eating tradition and not as the vegetarian fulfillment of Isaiah 11:1–9. This passage is crucial in Skriver's thought, as he believes it links the branch [*netser*] from the root of Jesse (11:1) and Isaiah's vegetarian vision (11:6–9) with New Testament references to Jesus being a Nazorean. This bit of textual gymnastics, along with the Essene hypothesis, proves for Skriver that Jesus must have been a vegetarian.

Have We Caught Anything?

The preceding section gives us an overview of the vegetarian Jesus literature. Now we must ask the questions, Do these authors pre-

sent a valid argument? and Why haven't their views been accepted by the academic community? Of course, we can dismiss the
forgeries, but what about Vaclavik, Ewing, and Skriver? Certainly,
the historical Jesus is a hot topic among biblical scholars. If these
authors have indeed found something worth pursuing, then it
would have been picked up by the academy. For some reason,
however, the approach to the historical Jesus taken by these
authors lacks scholarly credibility.

The problem in a nutshell is that they all suffer from uncritical
reading of source materials that are selectively gathered to support a preconceived thesis. Many of their key sources are historically questionable. Vaclavik, in particular, uncritically accepts historical material if it supports his presuppositions. Whatever is
contrary to his thesis he condemns as a corrupted text. Another
flaw with this genre, which is especially apparent in Ewing's writings, is dependence on outdated interpretations of the Dead Sea
materials. For example, Ewing claims that Jesus is the "Teacher of
Righteousness" mentioned in the Dead Sea Scrolls. This theory is
no longer held by scholars who work on the scrolls.

Another weakness in these writings is the common assumption
that Jesus was an Essene and that the Essenes were vegetarian.
The present academic consensus is that Jesus was not an Essene.
There are simply too many dissimilarities to establish identity. For
example, Jesus rejected ritual purity laws and practiced open
table fellowship (the Essenes would never eat with sinners and tax
collectors). Jesus' rejection of the purity laws is in marked contrast with the Essenes, who lived and breathed by the external
code. Violation of this cardinal Essene tenet in itself virtually
eliminates Jesus from being an Essene.

But weren't the Essenes vegetarian? First, if Jesus was not an
Essene, then the question is no longer relevant. Second, even if
Jesus was an Essene, excavations of the remains of ritual meals at
Qumran strongly imply that the Essenes who lived at the Dead
Sea community ate meat. One of their scrolls, the *Damascus
Document*, reads,

> No man shall defile himself by eating any live creature or creeping
> thing, from the larvae of bees to all creatures which creep in water.

They shall eat no fish unless split alive and their blood poured out. And as for locusts, according to their various kinds they shall plunge them alive into fire or water, for this is what their nature requires. (CD XII)

This text suggests that the Essenes were concerned with maintaining ceremonial purity, not with abstaining from flesh foods. It implies that any food permitted by Jewish dietary laws would be allowed. Another Dead Sea document, the *Temple Scroll*, repeatedly asserts that animal sacrifice for sin is an "eternal rule." The *Temple Scroll* contains numerous references granting permission to eat animal sacrifices and other clean animals, even away from the Temple (cf. 11QT 47, 52–53). The primary dietary concerns for the Essenes were ritual purity and moderation. The only food they could eat was food produced by the community, since they knew it had been grown and prepared according to Jewish dietary laws. Their ritual purity was intended to prepare a holy community for the Messiah.

Another central thesis in the vegetarian Jesus literature is the claim that the New Testament documents were edited to remove any traces of vegetarianism. There is, however, no textual or historical evidence to support this assumption. New Testament manuscripts that predate the supposed time of editing (around A.D. 325) show no signs of an original vegetarian text. Granted, there was some editing taking place, but of neither the magnitude nor subject matter that the vegetarian Jesus writers claim.

Moreover, there is no evidence that the church condemned vegetarianism. On the contrary, Christian asceticism flourished during this period. The church permitted ascetics and other Christians to practice vegetarianism as long as they did not denounce meat eating as evil. The church wanted to guard against the heresy of gnostic dualism (spirit is good; matter is evil). While the Council of Nicea did not mention vegetarianism, several other church synods and councils of the period did—and they all approved it as long as it was not done out of abhorrence for God's physical creation!

We must conclude that there is insufficient evidence to support a vegetarian Jesus. Although it cannot be verified, it would appear that Jesus at least ate fish. This conclusion raises insurmountable problems for ethical vegetarians and animal rights activists who seek religious backing for their views. How could Jesus, the paragon of moral perfection, possibly have condoned killing a living creature by eating its flesh? I would suggest that the problem is not so much with Jesus as it is with the mode of thinking that asks this kind of question, for it is still thinking in terms of the historical Jesus.

Casting the Net on the Other Side

Historical reconstructions have always been plagued with subjectivity and confusion, as witnessed by the endless array of Jesuses that creative minds have passed off on the public. Behind the modern quest to find Jesus' actual words and deeds lies the Enlightenment demand for objective and demonstrable grounds for faith and practice. If it can be "proven" that Jesus ate meat, we eat meat (the logic of many Christians); if it can be "proven" that Jesus abstained, we abstain (the logic of the vegetarian Jesus crowd). However, if it is discerned from historical research that Jesus probably ate fish and if this runs counter with what we consider moral probity, then we are in deep trouble (the argument to this point). But we should remind ourselves that an ethics based on a historical reconstruction is no more possible than the reconstruction itself.

The flaw in this kind of thinking is the assumption that Christian life and thought must be grounded on historical reconstructions of the life of Jesus rather than on the faith portraits of the remembered Jesus as we have received them. The Bible has always been the formative text that shapes Christian identity. God speaks to us today through God's Word, not through historical reconstructions. Reliance on the gospel portraits, however, once again confronts us with my friend's question, for Luke depicts Jesus as eating fish.

You're right, we're still in a pickle. The answer involves thinking critically within the realm of faith about what we have received. The faith portraits of Jesus include the incarnation and resurrection. While these elements of faith lie firmly nestled in the realm of mystery and far beyond rational proof, they provide a paradigm for partially coming to grips with the problem at hand. As the supreme paradox of the Christian faith, the incarnation cautions us against trying to understand divine action in the world and against expecting to comprehend fully why God incarnate, the Lord of all life, ate the flesh of dead animals.

Nevertheless, by exploring various implications of the incarnation and resurrection we can make overtures toward unraveling the dilemma of why the gospel portraits have Jesus eating fish. It is a foundational Christian belief that God through Christ entered into solidarity with fallen humanity, suffered with creation in a world less than perfect, and achieved victory over the forces of sin, evil, oppression, and death by the resurrection. Though not sinful himself, Christ assumed the fallen state to heal the fallen state. The following are a few reflections on these basic Christian affirmations that may be helpful.

First, since the biblical narrative depicts God as conceding the eating of meat (Gen 9:3), it must be regarded as morally neutral in Jesus' day when done without cruelty, in moderation, and in gratitude to the incomprehensible grace of God. The only impropriety associated with meat eating in the Jewish culture was consuming unclean animals (such as pigs) or overindulging. And it was into this culture that Christ entered.

Second, divine activity among humans invariably involves accommodation to human life and customs. Said another way, divine activity in a disordered world saturated with evil and violence must inevitably be less than ideal. The way things are is the context for God to invoke change. God participates in human history through a process of accommodation, a process in which God allows humans freedom and then works through that freedom and the customs which it spawns (such as wars, sacrifice, and meat eating) to achieve the divine goal. The God who cannot look upon evil (Hab 1:13) became incarnate in Christ and mingled with tax collectors and sinners.

Third, the circumstances in first-century Palestine are radically different than ours. Neither Jesus nor the gospel writers had to cope with the ethical problems of factory farms, animal abuse, and the like. They were simply not issues in first-century Palestine. The dietary issue Jesus confronted was the legalistic abuse of the food laws to obtain holiness. One always interprets the significance of the biblical narrative through the horizon of one's own context. Thus God may speak through the Word to Christians today in ways that God did not speak to the gospel writers in the first century.

Fourth, the primary focus of Christ's mission was to mend the estrangement between humanity and God; that is, to address the root problem of our disordered world. Forsaking the ways of God engenders wrong attitudes and dispositions which lead to environmental degradation as well as oppression and victimization of others, whether human or nonhuman. Before creation can be healed, humanity must be healed by returning to God. Jesus came to give his life a ransom for many (Mark 10:45) and to call sinners to repentance before a holy God (Luke 5:32). He did not come to legislate vegetarianism, animal rights, health reform, or end slavery.

Fifth, Christians have always been shaped by the patterns of meaning in the gospel portraits, not by the particulars. That is, Christians do not normally walk from town to town proclaiming the kingdom, overturn tables in the Temple, or preach from mountain tops. That is not what it means to follow Jesus. Rather than imitating Jesus in the particulars, following Jesus means being shaped by the patterns of meaning found in the gospel portraits. The two most prominent patterns are (1) Jesus' radical devotion and obedience to God and (2) Jesus' radical selfless love for others, even if this may mean death (Johnson, *The Real Jesus*, pp. 151–66). One cannot really follow the particulars since they differ from one gospel to another. However, by following the patterns as symbolized in Jesus' death, burial, and resurrection, we become cruciform people in giving ourselves to others—and today this may mean abstaining from animal flesh.

Sixth, Jesus himself suffered as a victim at the hands of the oppressors. In so doing he joined sides with all victimized creatures, both human and nonhuman. The story of a suffering creation finds meaning and hope only as it is located in the story of the suffering God, who out of love voluntarily assumed creaturely limitations and affliction. The cross gives consolation to those who suffer, and the resurrection is a victory over and a protest against injustice, oppression, victimization, and death. As we protest against animal cruelty, factory farms, and unnecessary animal experimentation, we do so in concert with God and in anticipation of the resurrection hope. The message of the risen Christ is a message of hope to all who suffer, both humans and animals.

Even with the above suggestions, the question Why? still lingers in our minds. We have not really explained why the faith portraits of Jesus have him eating fish. Why God had to became incarnate in Jesus Christ and accommodate the divine self to human customs is beyond our comprehension. This principle of accommodation is similar to Paul's statement in 1 Corinthians 9:22, "I have become all things to all people that I might by all means save some."

In the same way, God entered into solidarity with fallen humanity in order to bring salvation and renewal to a fallen world. The incarnation and divine accommodation are limit questions that bring us to the brink of human understanding. How can anyone fathom the love that impelled the infinite God to become finite and vulnerable? With Andrew Linzey we affirm that "to confess Christ crucified is to confess a Christ inevitably and profoundly limited by the fact of incarnation" (*Theology*, p. 87).

Why Jesus, as God incarnate and author of all life, ate the flesh of dead animals must therefore remain hidden in the mysterious ways of God. We do not understand why God has made or allowed the world to be as it is, with its predation, suffering, and death. Nor do we understand why Jesus condoned killing for food and partook of animal flesh. We may humbly question God in the spirit of the prophets and offer protests in view of the resurrection promise. However, in the end we must let God be God and not impose our conceptions and agendas upon the God of creation.

The observation that the gospels have Jesus eating fish lessens neither the spiritual nor ethical reasons for Christian vegetarianism, for Christians are followers of the crucified and risen Christ.

To confess the risen Christ is to testify of the present possibility of a new kind of existence for all creation—an existence without war, oppression, exploitation, and unnecessary killing. Christian vegetarianism is a protest against such abuses and a testimony of the cosmic reconciliation available through the transforming power of the risen Christ.

RECIPES

Broccoli Stroganoff

> 4 cups whole wheat flat noodles
> 1 bunch fresh broccoli
> Water for noodles and broccoli

Steam broccoli until tender. While broccoli is cooking, bring water to boil in a 3-quart saucepan for the noodles. When the water is boiling rapidly, drop noodles in water and cook for 12 minutes. The trick to preparing good whole wheat pasta is to keep the water boiling rapidly the entire cooking time. Serve the broccoli over the noodles and then top with Sunflower Sour Cream sauce (see below). This is a quick, easy, and very tasty meal. Could substitute frozen broccoli, frozen California vegetable blend, or other vegetables for the fresh broccoli.

Sunflower Sour Cream

> 1 cup raw sunflower seeds
> 1⅔ cups water
> 1 tsp. salt
> 1 tsp. onion powder
> 1 tsp. garlic powder
> ⅓ cup fresh lemon juice
> 1 Tbs. white flour

Blend all ingredients until smooth and creamy. The more you blend, the thicker it becomes. After using on the Broccoli Stroganoff, save rest to put on baked potatoes, Haystacks Unlimited (chapter 6), or Bean Burritos (chapter 7). To make an onion dip, add ¼ cup onion flakes and use ⅓ cup less water.

2

Would a Veggie Garfield Be a Happy Cat?

God said, "See, I have given you every plant yielding seed that is upon the face of all the earth, and every tree with seed in its fruit; you shall have them for food. And to every beast of the earth, and to every bird of the air, and to everything that creeps on the earth, everything that has the breath of life, I have given every green plant for food." (Genesis 1:29–30)

Love the animals: God has given them the rudiments of thought and joy untroubled. Do not trouble it, don't harass them, don't deprive them of their happiness, don't work against God's intent. Man, do not pride yourself on superiority to the animals; they are without sin, and you, with your greatness, defile the earth by your appearance on it, and leave the traces of your foulness after you—alas, it is true of almost everyone of us! (Fyodor Dostoevsky, *The Brothers Karamazov* VI.3g)

The clearest statement in the Bible regarding vegetarianism is Genesis 1:29–30. It speaks of vegetarianism not only for humans but also for animals! Wonder what the famous gourmand cat Garfield would think about such a confining regimen? Probably not much. But Garfield is not alone. What about all those epicurean humans who savor their hamburgers, barbecue ribs, and sirloin steaks? Does the Bible actually teach that we are supposed to be vegetarians? Have Christians ignored what the Bible says?

Most Christians respond by saying that the passage has been superseded by God's permission to eat meat in Genesis 9:3. But has our rollicking in God's permission caused us to overlook something in the Genesis 1 text? Why is the vegetarian passage in the Bible? How did it get there and what is it saying?

What Inspired the Veggie Passage?

The story of creation tells us something about the way God envisions the world to be. It depicts a community that was functioning in harmony with everything else and with its Creator—just the way God intended it to be. There were no homicide reports or obituary columns in the *Eden Gazette,* and all you could find at the local inn was a vegetarian fare. Biblical writers often draw upon the garden image as a metaphor of peace and harmony. The bountiful garden symbolizes a blessed state for all the earth in which violence, oppression, hatred, killing, disease, and death are totally absent (Isa 51:3; Ezek 36:35; Rev 21–22). Destruction of gardens in Scripture symbolizes disharmony in God's creation (Amos 4:9).

How did we get this story of beginnings? No human was there to record what was going on. A possible explanation is that it resulted from inspired reflections on God's delivering the children of Israel out of Egypt. What kind of God was it who delivered the Israelites out of bondage? Was it not a God who is concerned with peace and justice? Was it not a God who willingly becomes involved with creaturely life and who opposes violence, killing, oppression, and exploitation? Was it not a God of liberation? The exodus was indeed a revelatory event in which God revealed the divine self as a God who loves and cares for those who suffer.

The children of Israel had spent some 400 years as nonpersons in slavery to the Egyptians. Who were these liberated masses, aside from being nameless nomads with neither homeland nor identity? In addition to seeking a homeland in Canaan, the children of Israel also sought to express their identity. They knew who they were; they were a people delivered out of slavery by a loving and merciful God. This liberating God was all they had to cling on to. But how was this to be expressed? It was common practice for people in those days to identify themselves with the gods through creation stories. However, the creation stories in vogue at the time portrayed a pantheon of gods and goddesses of the worst sort—engaging in sexual perversion, cursing, aggression, war, killing, distrust, eating their own children, drunken orgies. This was not the God experienced by the Israelites.

The creation stories of these gods and goddesses would not do either, for they depicted creation as the result of sexual intercourse or a violent cosmic conflict. For example, the Babylonian creation myth *Enuma Elish* has Marduk (the sun god) chopping up Tiamat (the female goddess of chaos) and scattering her dismembered cadaver to form the world. The Babylonian myth depicts creation as an act of violence, where chaos is conquered by brutality. In contrast, reflections on the exodus revealed a significantly more majestic God (and God-given insight) than the unrefined and crude gods of the ancient Near East. The creation story that gave identity to the people of Israel had to be different—creation had to be an act of love, where peace and justice are maintained through compassion and kindness.

Divine insight led the children of Israel to make a very significant correlation: the loving Redeemer who had led them out of oppression is also the Creator who fashioned and cares for the entire creation. If God is both liberator and Creator, then God would want all creation to be liberated from oppression just like the Israelites were liberated. How could the God of the exodus ever sanction oppression against those of differing social standing, gender, race, or even species?

Another historical insight that helps us understand the creation stories is Israel's nomadic way of viewing life. In contrast to the Greeks, who searched history philosophically to find what is absolute and universal amid change, the Hebrews explored history prophetically to uncover new hopes and possibilities for the future amid suffering and oppression. The Greek mind looked for constants; the Hebrew mind for change. Owing to their nomadic heritage, the Israelites looked forward, not backwards. They were always on the move to a future that lay before them. It would be contrary to the Hebrew mind to think of returning to a former state of existence. Reflections on their liberation from oppression led the Israelites to formulate cosmic eschatological hopes. They understood the beginning and end only from the middle; that is, by interpreting the exodus as God's self-revelation in history. Jürgen Moltmann remarks that "in the Hebrew and Christian view of history the past is a promise to the future; consequently, the interpretation of the past becomes a prophecy in reverse" (p. 109).

In summary, the Israelites viewed the creation narratives primarily as a story of beginnings to give identity to their people and secondarily as a symbol of hope of a future age without oppression. This identity and hope was shaped by the revelatory event of the exodus. Recognizing God as both liberator and Creator suggests a God who desires cosmic deliverance with peace, justice, and integrity for all creation. The same God who created humans and animals seeks to liberate all humans and animals from oppression. Eden would then represent the hopes of universal peace and harmony that this elevated concept of God would inspire. An integral part of this vision is humanity's peaceful coexistence with nonhuman creation.

What Is the Veggie Passage Really Saying?

As Christians we listen to what the biblical narrative says, for it is the biblical narrative that shapes our identity. We often think and act differently from others because our lives have been molded by the Scriptures. But listening to the text often entails a close reading in light of its historical situation and literary context. And sometimes this is difficult. Is Genesis 1:29–30 really saying that vegetarianism is the expected norm for people (and animals) today? Is vegetarianism really the primary focus of the passage?

In the previous section we looked at the historical context of the passage. Now we must look at the literary context. Scholars say there are two creation stories: the Priestly creation tradition

(Gen 1:1–2:4a) and the Yahwist creation tradition (Gen 2:4b–3:24). They have been put together in such a way as to augment each other. The Priestly tradition speaks of cosmic creation and contains priestly concerns, such as God's resting on and hallowing the seventh day. The Yahwist tradition speaks of the creation and estrangement of humanity. It presents a different portrait of God and has more of a narrative quality compared to the hymnic quality of Genesis 1.

The first creation story is cosmic in scope and is constructed around the seven days of creation. Of particular concern for us is the sixth day of creation, which can be divided into three sections: (1) God creates humans in the divine image and gives them dominion over the earth (1:26–28); (2) God announces a vegetarian diet for humans and animals (1:29–30); (3) God observes that all things are very good (1:31).

Whatever the vegetarian passage means, it must somehow tie in with the passages before and after it. The exact meaning of the divine image is debatable, but in light of the exodus experience it may have something to do with our moral intuition that peace and justice are right and that oppression and violence are wrong. Interwoven with God's creating humans in the divine image is God's granting dominion. The close connection of these two ideas implies that "dominion" refers to the care and governance of creation in accord with the divine image—without any exploitation, violence, and oppression. The image of God would then serve as a pattern for our dominion. The psalmists understand God as exercising dominion over creation with compassion and loving kindness (cf. Ps 72:8–14; 145:8–21). It is a dominion in which the stronger not only helps, nourishes, protects, and cares for the weaker but also shows compassion, kindness, and mercy.

Then comes the vegetarian passage, which, by the way, was written by those who were anything but vegetarian! The vegetarian passage tells how the dominion was to be carried out—it was to be without killing or exploiting any living creature. Moltmann writes,

> To "subdue the earth" refers to the nourishment of human beings, which according to vv. 29 and 30, is evidently supposed to be exclu-

sively vegetarian. . . . This means that the right to kill animals is excluded from the lordship of human beings over them. If human beings and animals alike eat vegetarian food, then the "lordship" of human beings over animals can mean no more than that human beings have the function of a "justice of the peace." (*God in Creation*, Fortress, 1993, p. 224)

The vegetarian passage then speaks of peace and harmony throughout creation, and the dominion passage speaks of God's desire for humans to maintain this orderly state of affairs as far as humanly possible and to treat all life with respect.

Taking a closer look at the passage, we note two kinds of permitted food. First, some food comes from plants yielding seed. The Hebrew word for "plants" is a general word for annuals, such as grass, grains, vegetables. In Psalm 102:4 the word is used as a symbol of transitoriness. But was the entire plant eaten or only the seed or fruit? The modifying phrase "yielding seed" could simply serve to distinguish these plants from those that reproduce vegetatively. This would allow the whole plant to be eaten. However, the similar expression in the next phrase regarding trees implies that only the seed or fruit part was eaten. Thus it seems probable that the passage refers to the grains and fruits of annual seed-bearing plants.

Second, some food comes from trees that bear seeded fruit. As mentioned above, it is assumed that only the fruit of the trees is meant (e.g., apricots, olives, figs, dates, pomegranates). Nuts would also be considered a seeded fruit. Although not exactly trees, we probably should include the fruit from berry bushes and vines in this category (e.g., blackberries, grapes). It appears then that the Edenic diet was conceived as consisting of grains, seeds, nuts, legumes, and fruits, or what is commonly called a "fruitarian" diet. Some suggest that humans were restricted to a fruitarian diet because it did not require killing the plant.

But should we understand the vegetarian passage literally as an ethical norm for people today or as a composite image anticipating peace and harmony throughout creation? The historical and literary context strongly suggests that the primary intent is to convey a composite image or symbol of creation peace. If this is the case, should we press the details? Is vegetarianism supposed to be proper diet for humans?

Several years ago while teaching college I used to jest with my students about their meat-eating habits, just as they jested with me about my vegetarianism. My favorite retort was, "Well, in the beginning, it wasn't so." Was I pressing the literal too far? But then, if it symbolizes peace and harmony, does that mean we can totally forget the particulars? No, not really. There is still something there that we must grapple with. The vegetarian motif corresponds to virtually every salvation text in Scripture by envisioning community without violence. Salvation would be an inconceivable paradox if killing of any kind continues.

"But this is impossible," you say. "The only life we know is one in which life is possible only at the death of something else. Since this seems to be an inescapable reality, why not kill for food?" The Bible, however, is fairly consistent in setting before us a hope that contradicts everything we know about life. What are we to do— believe only what is rationally verifiable or place our hope in the impossible possibilities of God? As people of hope, we cannot easily dismiss what the Bible says about a time free of killing and death. To be honest, we don't know exactly what this means. Nor do we know the full implications of Christ's resurrection, but the belief that somehow the resurrection answers the problems of violence, oppression, killing, and death shapes the way we think and act. It is a belief that challenges us to take the vegetarian motif in Genesis a bit more seriously.

But Garfield Was Not Made for Eating Grass

A veggie Garfield? You've got to be kidding. Garfield's large canines would surely get in the way and make hash of the straw. It is a perplexing question. Why were dogs and cats created with large canines and short intestinal tracts if they were intended to be vegetarian? All vegetarian animals have short canines and long intestinal tracts. The question, however, goes beyond the intent of the passage by presuming scientific precision of primeval history. As we have noted, the creation stories came into existence through divinely inspired reflections on God's self-revelation in the exodus. In other words, they are theological reflections, not scientific treatises.

Those who play the gambit and venture solutions to the riddle come up with some interesting, albeit dubious answers, none of which are really satisfying. Perhaps God changed the anatomy and instincts of carnivores after the fall. Or perhaps they evolved from the way God created them so as to survive. Christian faith and practice, however, are shaped by the biblical narrative, not by speculations. While it is impossible to scientifically explain the origins of life, we should leave open the possibility that creation was somewhat less than perfect and had a few more rough edges than many commonly think. Nevertheless, what we can affirm is that God, as Maker of heaven and earth, is active among us to liberate creation from its bondage.

If we view the creation stories from the perspective of the ancient Israelites rather than from the modern rationalistic point of view that demands scientific and historical precision, we would have much less difficulty with the carnivore problem. We would recognize that the Bible was not intended as a textbook on history or science, but rather as inspired testimonies and reflections on the divine presence among God's people. What we find in the first creation narrative, as Claus Westermann says, is praise for a loving and majestic Creator and "a reverent concern to guard the inaccessible mystery of creation from the human attempt to describe it" (p. 173).

But what about the design of humans? Many have called attention to the similarities between humans and herbivores. First, herbivores (and humans) have relatively long intestines, whereas carnivores have relatively short intestines. The short intestines in carnivores allow for the quick passage of toxins, decaying flesh, cholesterol, and other potentially harmful substances present in flesh foods. The long intestines in herbivores provide the time needed to absorb nutrients from vegetable foods.

Second, the teeth of herbivores are large and flat, and their jaws are capable of a circular, grinding motion that is needed to chew vegetable foods. On the other hand, the sharp pointed teeth of carnivores are well-suited to tear flesh, but ill-suited to cut and chew vegetable foods. Their jaws only function in an up and down motion.

Third, vegetable foods require different bacteria to break them down than do flesh foods. The saliva of herbivores contains the enzyme ptyalin to help break down starches in plant foods. Carnivores lack this enzyme. Instead they secrete much more hydrochloric acid into their digestive tract than herbivores in order to dissolve bone material in their diet. Foods suited for carnivores therefore are not ideally suited for herbivores and vice versa. Although there is some debate on the issue, most agree that the anatomy and physiology of humans correspond more to herbivores than carnivores. From this analogy it is commonly argued that God created humans to be herbivores and that the natural diet for humans is vegetarian, a conclusion that corresponds to Genesis 1:29.

What do we make of all this? Are we not falling into the same "argument from design" pitfall that we ran into trying to figure out why Garfield has canines? Or is there something to it? Yes, there is certainly something to it. But rather than using these observations to "prove" the way things were in the beginning, it would be wiser to urge people today to eat foods that are healthier for the body and that the body better assimilates. It is rather clear that humans are much better at consuming and digesting plant foods. But if we persist in playing the game to establish divine intent from anatomical and physiological design, we will have detoured from the biblical narrative and will invariably run into the snag of Garfield's canines.

Does Garfield Have a Soul?

You may be wondering what Garfield's soul (or lack of it) has to do with vegetarianism. The answer in a nutshell—plenty. To unravel the question about souls in animals, we must once again delve into the Hebrew way of thinking. There is a certain Hebrew word that keeps cropping up in the creation stories. It is the word *nephesh*. *Nephesh* occurs in Genesis 1:20, 21, 24, and 30 to describe animals as "living creatures" or as having "the breath of life." The word is also used in reference to humans. In Genesis 2:7 God breathed into Adam the breath of life, and Adam became a "living being [*nephesh*]."

Nephesh is variously translated in the Hebrew Scriptures, all of which can be subsumed under the general category of that which makes people and animals animated living beings: personality, individuality, desire, life, mood or state of mind, feeling, volition. One of the more common translations of *nephesh* is "soul." It is not altogether inappropriate to say that animals have souls, if we understand "soul" as that quality that makes people and animals animated beings. The use of the word in reference to animals suggests that the Israelites recognized that animals have thoughts, feelings, emotions, desires, and self-awareness similar to those of humans.

The popular notion of soul in Christian theology, however, restricts it to the immaterial aspect of humans that enables them to have communion with God and to experience salvation. Animals, it is said, do not possess souls and cannot be saved. Therefore, since their eternal destiny is not at stake, it does not matter if we kill them. Although this idea has been pervasive throughout church history, it is difficult to support from the Bible. The common Christian notion of soul has actually come from Greek philosophy. Plato taught the immortality of the soul, and Aristotle added that only the rational soul was immortal and that only humans possessed it. This Aristotelian idea was picked up by Aquinas and has become part of the doctrine of the church.

The implication would be that there is no difference between animals and rocks or trees. The nonhuman world lies outside the realm of God's salvific intent and outside the realm of moral obligation and could thus be treated as commodities or resources to exploit. Although these ideas have served as a construct for Christian theology for centuries, they appear contradictory to many biblical texts and stand in need of revision.

The Bible teaches that (1) animals posses *nephesh* (Gen 1:20, 21, 24, 30, 2:19, 9:4–5, 10, 12, 15; Lev 24:18; Job 12:10; Prov 12:10); (2) animals possess *psuchē*, the Greek counterpart to *nephesh* in the New Testament (Rev 8:9, 16:3); (3) animals have an affinity for God (Ps 148:7–10, 150:6); (4) animals will be present in the eternal state (Isa 65:25; Rev 5:13–14); (5) humans are similar to animals in that they share the same breath or spirit *(ruach)* and the same destiny (Eccl 3:18–21); (6) animals await glorification as do the children of God (Rom 8:18–21); and (7) the redeeming purposes of God include the entire created realm, including animals (Eph 1:10; Col 1:20). David praises God saying, "You save humans and animals alike, O Lord" (Ps 36:6).

The Hebrew mind certainly associated animals and humans more closely than we moderns do. We don't exactly know what this immaterial aspect of humans is that we keep on calling "soul," but whatever it is, it does seem plausible that it is not the exclusive property of humans. Thus the lack of a soul can no longer be pressed into service as a justification for exploiting or abusing animals. Rather, the creation stories suggest that both animals and humans possess the animating life principle called *nephesh*. Plants do not possess *nephesh*. The diet prescribed for all creatures having a *nephesh* (or breath of life) did not include killing and eating other creatures with a *nephesh*. This implies that there is something special or sacred about the life principle *nephesh*.

According to the Hebrew way of thinking, it is the similarity between humans and animals that governs our conduct towards animals, not the differences. Animals are not objects for our exploitation; they are special creatures who also possess the mysterious quality of animated life. This cuts through any egotistical, prejudicial hubris that seeks to draw lines of ethical obligation on the basis of supposed differences, such as possessing an eternal soul, having reasoning or language abilities, or being made in the image of God. The question is not, Can they reason? nor, Can they talk? nor, Can they suffer? nor, Were they made in the image of God? but, Do they possess a *nephesh*? Possession of a *nephesh* is, unquestionably, the biblical criterion for establishing a compassionate ethic toward animals.

Yes, if Garfield heard all this, he would be a happy cat. And his favorite dishes, such as lasagna, could all be made the vegetarian way. Most important of all, Garfield and all Garfield's animal friends (and foes) would find hope in the images of Eden and refuge in the loving care of those who follow the risen Christ in protest against oppression, exploitation, violence, and killing.

RECIPES

Tofu Lasagna

>   1 medium chopped onion
>   1 16-oz. package of chopped spinach
>   1 recipe "Cheese" Sauce (see below)
>   1 28-oz. can crushed tomatoes
>   2 tsp. Italian seasoning
>   8 oz. whole wheat lasagna noodles (do not precook)
>   1 lb. tofu
>   ½ tsp. each garlic powder, onion powder, basil, salt
>   1 tsp. parsley flakes
>   3 Tbs. nutritional yeast flakes (this is food yeast, NOT
>   baking yeast or brewer's yeast; be sure to get flakes
>   fortified with vitamin B12)
>   ½ cup sliced olives

In a 3-quart saucepan sauté the onions in a small amount of water, adding the spinach to help it thaw out. Then mix onions and spinach together and drain well. Meanwhile, prepare cheese sauce. Add Italian seasoning to the can of crushed tomatoes. Then in a bowl crumble up tofu along with garlic and onion powder, basil, salt, parsley, and yeast flakes.

Layer as follows: **(1) Tomato.** Spread ½ cup crushed tomatoes on the bottom of a 13x9-inch baking dish. **(2) Noodles.** Arrange the first layer of uncooked lasagna noodles on top of the tomatoes. **(3)**

Tofu. Spread ½ of the tofu mixture over the noodles. **(4) Onion-Spinach.** Spread ½ of the onion-spinach mixture over tofu. **(5) Cheese.** Spread ⅔ cup "Cheese" Sauce over onion-spinach mixture. Repeat steps 1 through 5. Top with noodles, then rest of the crushed tomatoes, rest of the "Cheese" Sauce, and sliced olives. Bake at 375° for 1 hour. Let stand about 15 minutes before serving.

"Cheese" Sauce

⅓ cup raw sunflower seeds (or cashew pieces)
¼ cup nutritional yeast flakes
3 Tbs. cornstarch
1 Tbs. lemon juice
1½ tsp.salt
1 tsp. onion powder
½ tsp. garlic powder
1 4-oz. jar pimentos
2 cups water

Blend all ingredients until smooth. Cook in saucepan to thicken, stirring often. Great over vegetables, such as broccoli and baked potatoes, in casseroles, on toasted cheese sandwiches, in Macaroni and "Cheese" (chapter 11), and much more.

3

Was God
the First Tanner?

And the Lord God made garments of skins for the man and for his wife, and clothed them. (Genesis 3:21)

We may find it difficult to formulate a human right of tormenting beasts in terms which would not equally imply an angelic right of tormenting men. And we may feel that though objective superiority is rightly claimed for man, yet that very superiority ought partly to consist in not behaving like a vivisector: that we ought to prove ourselves better than the beasts precisely by the fact of acknowledging duties to them which they do not acknowledge to us. . . . If we cut up beasts simply because they cannot prevent us and because we are backing our own side in the struggle for existence, it is only logical to cut up imbeciles, criminals, enemies, or capitalists for the same reasons. (C. S. Lewis, "Vivisection," in *God in the Dock*, Eerdmans, 1970, pp. 226–27)

In the summer of 1995 a friend invited me to attend the National Alliance for Animals Annual Symposium in Washington, D.C. One drizzly morning before the conference sessions began, several hundred conference attendees traveled by chartered buses from the Dulles Marriott to the U.S. Capitol building to stage a protest demonstration. The government had been subsidizing mink farm operations to the tune of more than $1.94 million dollars annually. One of the recipients of this money was a mink farm in Maryland that was illegally killing the animals by injecting into their hearts the weed-killer Black Leaf 40. The weed killer paralyzed their lungs and commenced their prolonged and agonizing death by suffocation. The energetic demonstrators gathered on the steps of the Capitol building, chanted slogans, lifted signs and banners, and gave speeches, all rather peacefully and orderly. I was given a sign to lift above my head as we chanted that had a large picture of a mink with the words, STOP MINK FARM SUBSIDIES. The demonstration, which was staged by PETA (People for the Ethical Treatment of Animals), turned out to be successful, as Congress did not pass the renewal for the subsidy.

But why would an evangelical Christian want to participate in such demonstrations? Did not God give humans dominion over animals, delivering them over to us for food, clothing, and whatever? Not one word is mentioned in the Bible against animals being used for making tents, clothing, weapons, shofars (trumpets made out of ram's horns), wineskins, or bone tools. All of this would have involved suffering and death. And to top it off, God made garments from animal skins for Adam and Eve before sending them from the garden. If God was indeed the first tanner, then how could a Christian possibly object to animals being used for clothing, experimentation, and the like?

How Could God Do That?

We begin our inquiry by engaging the text in a careful reading, listening to what it is saying in light of its historical and literary contexts. The passage about God's making clothing for Adam and Eve from the skins of animals is part of the Yahwist tradition and comes at the end of the fall story that concludes the second creation narrative (Gen 2:4b–3:24). These thoughts resulted from growing strands of tradition that developed over time as pious Jews framed their reflections of their Redeemer God and the human predicament in a narrative, saga-like fashion.

The Yahwist creation narrative consists of two strands. The first strand is the creation of humans (2:4b–25). The second strand (the fall story) expresses humanity's depraved and alienated state (3:1–24). The narrative as a whole could be thought of as divinely inspired reflections on the existential questions of why humans who have been created by God find themselves estranged from God and why they are subject to sin, suffering, and death. In addition to portraying the human predicament, the story provides the background for the unfolding narrative of God's activity with the human race.

The fall story should be viewed more as a departure from the path leading toward God's goal for creation (i.e., the peaceable kingdom) than a departure from a chronologically prior perfect and static state. This interpretation follows that of the early church father Irenaeus (c. 130–200), who taught that paradise was only the first stage in humanity's growth toward maturity. Since the creature cannot be perfect like the Creator, the divine image reflected by Adam and Eve must be less than the divine exemplar and must allow space for development. This would mean that humans were not created mature or perfect but were like children created with the capacity to grow into conformity to the divine will and nature (*Against Heresies* 4.38.1). The fall represents a sidetrack into sin on the path toward maturity, a fork going down the wrong road. This fork in the road is graphically illustrated by God's expelling humans from the garden.

The notion of sin has fallen on hard ground lately. This is probably due to its being regarded as a violation of absolute rules which are then used to manipulate by fear in an aborted effort to force holiness upon an audience. Viewing sin in this way quickly leads to a quagmire of ethical confusion. Our story says that wrongdoing is primarily located in the heart; Eve *desired* to go beyond the divinely established boundaries and partake from the fruit for food and wisdom. That is, there was something amiss within before there was anything amiss without. What we are talking about are inner vices that lead us down the wrong path.

The story tells us that humans were driven by self-centered vices and were more interested in going their own way than following God's path. The detour was going to be a rather rough, and, yes, cursed road—and it may not even go through. So what does God do? Does God condemn humanity to outer darkness? No. God provides for their journey! "Incredible," you say. But that's not all. God's provision involved killing animals and making clothing out of their skins. "Doubly incredible. It doesn't look as if even God is much interested in reaching the peaceable kingdom." The key to understanding our dilemma is to understand that the loving and merciful God wants to travel with us and bless us on whatever path we choose. Why? Because by traveling with us God can lovingly woo us to join the procession toward the promised future. God always meets us where we are—and this is exactly what is happening in our text.

God's suiting them with leather garments was not done to hide their private parts, since the fig leaves would have been adequate. Then why the Davy Crockett outfits? Many suggest that the fig leaves were not adequate to cover their inward shame and guilt. These could only be covered by the shed blood of another. It is then asserted that God's action prefigures the sacrifice of Christ. However, this hardly fits the context. The rugged clothing most likely expresses God's continuing concern and care for humans despite their departure from God's ways. God had not abandoned the human race because of its sin. The fragile fig leaves would not be adequate protection along the rigorous and harsh path they had chosen.

But does this mean that God sanctions the slaying of animals for clothing? We should keep in mind what we have before us. The text consists of later reflections by pious Israelites about God's faithful provisions in spite of their waywardness. As such, it employs the customs of a semi-nomadic culture, which involved using animals for clothing, tents, tools, and food. How else could God's care for nomads be expressed other than providing the necessities of life in terms they could understand? As we will see in the next chapter, the Yahwist tradition often reads later customs back into primeval history. Also we should not forget John Calvin's insight that God accommodates divine revelation to human customs and modes of expression.

Thus we should understand the passage as later reflections about God's continuing care as we stumble along our ill-chosen path. It is through such inspired reflections that God reveals the divine self and speaks to us today. The reflections were framed as a saga using a common genre of the time. We can always listen to a text better if we know what kind of literature it is; we listen to poetry as poetry, history as history, and the like. With a saga-like narrative, we listen for the message it was intended to convey. Our ill-chosen path has taken us through some pretty rough times and into the repulsive situation we face today regarding animal abuse. Amid all these abominations, God remains with us, coaxing and wooing us onto the path toward the kingdom.

Did Adam Eat Meat after the Fall?

Before expelling the humans from the garden, God not only made them garments from animal skins but also told them what they should eat. One would expect that after the fall they would be allowed to eat meat. But this is not the case. Instead, God reiterated to Adam that he was still to have a vegetarian diet: "and you shall eat the plants of the field . . . until you return to the ground" (Gen 3:18–19). Even though living off the land would be more difficult along the hapless path they had chosen, Adam was still not permitted to kill animals for food.

The Hebrew word for "plants" in Genesis 3:18 is the same word which occurs in Genesis 1:29. As mentioned in chapter 2, it is a collective noun referring to annual plants, such as grass, grains, and vegetables. The difference between the reference in Genesis 1 and the one in Genesis 3 lies in the modifying phrases. Instead of "plant yielding seed" we now have "plants of the field." If we are correct in assuming that Genesis 1:29 refers only to grain, seeds, and fruit, then Genesis 3:18 may possibly refer to the vegetative parts of the plants. The "plants of the field" would then refer to coarse vegetables, such as leaves (spinach, lettuce, kale), stems (celery, rhubarb), roots (carrots, beets), tubers (potatoes, yams), and bulbs (onions, garlic).

The primary significance of the "after the fall" vegetarian diet is that it reveals the Israelites' divinely inspired belief and hope that a vegetarian diet is still possible amid a world of sin. Human society's being saturated with exploitation, violence, injustice, and oppression is no reason that we should not strive toward the Judeo-Christian hope of peace and justice throughout creation. The Israelites believed it was possible, at least individually, to attain a semblance of Edenic harmony in a sin-ridden world. This is especially noteworthy in that these reflections arise out of a nonvegetarian society. It is simply not what one would expect.

What about Modern-Day Tanners?

The story about God's making clothing for the humans out of animal skins does cause us to reflect a moment on what is happening today in the fur industry as well as in animal laboratories and the entertainment business. It is important not only to listen to the diverse voices in Scripture but also to the diverse voices of our day as we assess what God would have us do. Of the two sets of voices, the church has traditionally held that the biblical narrative, properly understood, is the controlling element.

We must listen—this time not to voices of a human language, but to the cries of our suffering co-creatures. For the most part, we do not hear the voices, for they have been conveniently removed from public scrutiny. Most would rather have it that way. They would rather not listen. They enjoy buying their leather belts and shoes at the mall, cosmetics at the drugstore, and steaks at the supermarket without hearing anything. But the silenced voices are not really silent. Out of the deadening silence of the fur racks, shoe departments, and meat counters comes a symphony of voices that wanted to live and enjoy life the same as we do. A sensitive ear can hear the squeals and bellowing that accompanied the last agonizing moments of their existence, as well as the pain and frustration they suffered most of their miserable, forlorn, and dejected lives. It is to these forgotten voices we now turn.

Sometimes the voices from the animal experimentation laboratories appear rather mute, as in the case of mice and rats which are not noticeably expressive when in pain or in the case of pound-seizured dogs whose vocal cords have been severed. And then there are the rabbits, birds, guinea pigs, hamsters, farm animals, chimpanzees, and cats. But these are not the only voices. We have all heard the voices telling us about the good that has been accomplished, such as the polio vaccination. Yes, we should listen to these voices too, and listening does complicate the picture. We would like to find cures for AIDS and cancer. However, animal research is rather dubious at best. The assumed similarity between animals and humans has often led scientists down the wrong path. How an animal responds to a certain chemical does not always mimic how humans will respond. This has caused many scientists to conclude that animal experimentation is not an accurate and reliable means of medical research. Our point is not to argue the pros and cons on the issue, but to listen to the suffering—to that other voice which many have not heard before.

Approximately twenty million animals are used each year for research in the United States and one hundred million globally. The animals are injected with chemicals, burned, irradiated, fed large quantities of drugs, potential carcinogens, and toxicants (e.g., cleaning fluids), dismembered, shocked with electric current, crippled by severing the spinal cord, infected with diseases (e.g., cancer, AIDS), squirted in the eye with chemical substances, forced to inhale fumes of burning substances, and the like, almost always without pain killers. These animals are routinely used to evaluate whether new products (from shampoos to weed killers) would in any way be harmful to humans—by irritating the eyes or skin, causing toxic poisoning, cancer, birth defects, or other ailments. Animals are also used in an attempt to learn more about diseases and to find cures and treatments. Some experiments appear overly frivolous, such as testing cosmetic products and analyzing psychological behavior. After experiments are finished, the animals are routinely killed.

The Lethal Dose 50 Percent (LD-50) test determines how much dosage it takes to kill 50 percent of the test animals. This is a highly controversial test because of the suffering inflicted on animals and the unreliability of the results. Since the dosages needed to kill closely related animals varies drastically, the test has dubious relevance to humans. What may be toxic to animals may not be toxic to humans, and vice versa. To obtain these dubious results animals often undergo a period of severe convulsing because of the force-fed chemicals.

Another procedure is the Draize Eye-Irritancy test. It is used to test various household products and cosmetics. The substance is sprayed or applied some other way to one eye of an albino rabbit. Rabbits are commonly used because they are inexpensive, docile, and have large eyes. The rabbits are constrained in devices that immobilize them and expose their heads through a collar. Normally no pain killer is given. However, since rabbit eyes are quite different from human eyes, the results do not necessarily indicate how humans would react.

To present a balanced picture, we should note that medical research offers incredible potential that very few would want to curtail. To glean the best of both worlds, there have been attempts to relieve unnecessary suffering and continue research at the same time. Some laboratories have constructed mazes and hiding places to imitate natural habitats for their mice and rats. This would tend to alleviate some of the environmental and emotional stress. Work is also underway to develop alternative procedures to replace animal testing. The 1985 amendment to the Animal Welfare Act and the 1985 Health Research Extension Act both encourage research into alternative methods. For example, the CAM test in which egg membrane reacts with toxic substances is a possible replacement for the Draize Eye-Irritancy test. The picture is changing. Yet there is still much suffering. While there is no accurate way of measuring pain in animals, the privation, discomfort, stress, and frustration of most animals used in experiments are rather obvious.

While not as high on the public awareness charts, the fur and animal entertainment industries also have their problems. The disturbing thing about them is that neither one is necessary. There are plenty of alternative clothing articles on the market made from natural or synthetic fibers to replace animal furs and hides. There are also plenty of alternate forms of entertainment. We can drastically reduce animal suffering simply by being wise consumers. Our purpose for the moment, however, is simply to become aware of the problems so as to allow God to speak to us in our present context through the biblical narrative.

The infamous steel jaw leghold trap which is used to catch wild animals is still legal in the United States, even though it has been banned in over 65 countries. A bill to ban the trap was introduced in 1995, but it failed to pass (several states have banned it). The trap clamps onto the animal's leg with crushing force, leaving the animal lying crippled and in pain sometimes for days or weeks until the trapper arrives for the kill. The animals are commonly killed by beating with a blunt instrument, stomping on the chest, or drowning, so as not to damage the fur. Sometimes the animals bite off their trapped limb in order to escape. According to a 1989 HSUS report, seventeen million wild animals are trapped each year in the United States, most by the leghold trap. This includes foxes, wolves, coyotes, raccoons, bobcats, beavers, muskrats, otters, and minks. Another unfortunate aspect of traps is that they are indiscriminate, potentially snaring domestic animals and children. An estimated five million non-target animals are killed yearly by various kinds of traps.

Animals are also commonly used for entertainment, from cockfighting (illegal in many states) to horse racing, rodeos, and circuses. Circus animals in particular suffer anxiety, behavioral stress, trauma, boredom, and frustration when forced to live contrary to their nature and deprived of their basic physical, social, and psychological needs. They spend long hours in cramped cages or on chains, being let loose only to perform or train. Between shows they travel long hours confined in railroad boxcars. Reports of physical abuse and neglect among circus animals surface frequently, especially about harsh discipline involving beating elephants. But then elephants can be very dangerous to audiences if they break loose. They do need to be contained. It is a difficult situation, but it is one humans have created and put the animals into. Again, while we cannot accurately access the degree of animal suffering, it is beyond question that circus animals do suffer needlessly in various ways in order that humans can be amused.

Do Animals Have Rights?

If animals have the basic rights to live and enjoy life, then it would become a moral issue to use them for food, clothing, entertainment, or experiments. It would mean that humans are under a moral obligation to limit their own freedom and to respect those rights. Ethical vegetarians usually argue for vegetarianism on the basis of animal rights. Most Christians recoil at the thought of animal rights, primarily because of the received Western tradition which gives humans uncontested jurisdiction over animals. However, in view of our present situation we do need to interact with the notion of rights. Andrew Linzey has offered a useful Christian approach to animal rights based on theos-rights (*Rights*, pp. 68–98; and *Theology*, pp. 19–27). The following are some of my own reflections on this basic idea.

First, ultimately only God has rights. God loves and cares for creation and has the right to expect this loving care be replicated by humans. Creation exists, not for the glory of humanity, but for the glory of God. God has the right to see that earthly creatures are free to live according to their nature and without unnecessary abuse, exploitation, and pain, so that their lives can glorify their Creator.

Second, animals and humans have rights, but only in so far as they are derived from God's rights. Hence, God's creatures have a derived right to live a natural life and to be loved, cared for, and protected against abuse and exploitation. Said another way, since God values and cares for all creation, creation has a derived right to be valued and cared for by humans for God's glory.

Third, derived rights are not absolute. They can be revoked if abused. For example, God has given humans and animals the gift of life and the right to enjoy it. Yet "when an ox gores a man or a woman to death, the ox shall be stoned, and its flesh shall not be eaten" (Exod 21:28). The ox has forfeited its right to life. Very few would question that imprisoning a chronic serial killer violates his rights.

Fourth, derived rights reflect the ideal. God is amazingly patient about the ideals being formed in our lives and has even allowed such things as meat eating and animal sacrifice. We often forget about divine patience when we demand and absolutize where God does not. Rather than the static god of Greek philosophy, the God of the Bible is quite flexible and has entered into a dynamic give-and-take relationship with humanity due to the complexities of the fallen state. God lovingly encourages us toward the ideal rather than imposing binding laws upon us. This cautions us against reducing rights to absolute rules.

Fifth, conflicts in rights need to be worked out through love. By removing the absolutism often attached to rights, we have partially dissipated the wars that often take place between conflicting parties and opened up the possibility of peaceable resolutions. By refusing to demand our "rights," we have allowed space for the basic Christian virtue of love to inform our decisions. Rights then are guidelines for the journey which are to be worked out in specific cases through the sacrificial love of Christ. This move retains the notion of rights but shifts it from functioning under a rule-based ethic to functioning under a character-based ethic that is shaped by the biblical narrative.

Closing Thought

Unlike the Israelite society from which our text arose, we live in a society in which technology has liberated us from the need to use animals for food, clothing, and other items the ancients could obtain no other way. With the development of natural and synthetic fabrics, there is no reason any longer to kill animals for durable clothing (e.g., shoes, coats, belts). The medical picture is a bit more complex. But let me close with a haunting quotation from Andrew Linzey that reflects the virtue of self-sacrificial love (*Rights*, pp. 124–25):

> One *Christian* answer to these questions has yet to be heard. It is that, deeply conscious of our divinely given stewardship over creation and our special bond of covenant with animals in particular, we should

elect to bear for ourselves whatever ills may flow from not experimenting on animals rather than be supporting an institution which perpetuates tyranny. This may be a hard option for many, but it is as arguably a Christian response as many of the others which claim that appellation. If it is the *good* shepherd as opposed to the hireling who actually lays down his life for the sheep, perhaps the *good* steward is the one who desists from any path of injury in deference to the prior right of God in creation.

R E C I P E S

Vegetarian Chili

> 1 lb. package dried kidney beans
> 8 cups water (for soaking)
> 6 cups fresh water
> 1 cup diced green peppers
> 1 cup chopped onion
> 4 to 6 garlic cloves
> 1 28-oz. can crushed tomatoes
> 2 tsp. each cumin, onion powder
> 1½ tsp. salt
> 1 tsp. each paprika, garlic powder, basil,
>   brown sugar

Sort and rinse beans, then soak them overnight in large pot with 8 cups water. Next day, drain, rinse, and cook beans in 6 cups fresh water for 1½ hours. Then add the rest of ingredients and cook for at least 1 more hour, stirring occasionally. Great with cornbread. **Variations:** Could add 2 tsp. chili powder and 2 chopped tomatoes. Could also add 1 cup TVP (textured vegetable protein). Prepare the TVP by combining with ¾ cup water and heating in a frying pan. Then add to the chili with the rest of the ingredients.

Soybean Cornbread

⅔ cup soybeans
2 cups water to soak soybeans
¼ cup each rolled oats and brown sugar
2 tsp. salt
2 cups fresh water
2 cups cornmeal (can substitute some yellow corn grits)

Sort and rinse beans, then soak them overnight in 2 cups water. Next day, preheat the oven to 400°, put 2 cups of cornmeal in a large mixing bowl, and rub some oil and lecithin in an 8x8-inch baking dish. Then drain water from the soybeans and put them in a blender along with the oats, sugar, salt, and 2 cups of fresh water. Thoroughly blend the soybean mixture until smooth. Then pour the mixture into the cornmeal, stir together, and pour into the 8x8-inch baking dish. Bake at 400° for 40 minutes.

4

Was Noah's Ark an Early Food Factory?

The Lord said to Noah, "Go into the ark. . . . Take with you seven pairs of all clean animals, the male and its mate; and a pair of the animals that are not clean, the male and its mate; and seven pairs of the birds of the air also, male and female, to keep their kind alive on the face of all the earth." (Genesis 7:1–3)

Wherever an animal is in any way forced into the service of man, every one of us must be concerned with the sufferings which for that reason it has to undergo. . . . No one must shut his eyes and regard as non-existent the sufferings of which he spares himself the sight. Let no one regard as light the burden of his responsibility. While so much ill-treatment of animals goes on, while the moans of thirsty animals in railway trucks sound unheard, while so much brutality prevails in our slaughter-houses, . . . while animals have to endure intolerable treatment from heartless men, or are left to the cruel play of children, we all share the guilt. (Albert Schweitzer, *Philosophy of Civilization*, Macmillan, 1949, pp. 318–19)

Very few people visit slaughterhouses. It is simply not a place one goes for entertainment. However, the Russian novelist and social reformer Leo Tolstoy was one of those venturesome souls who did. Tolstoy had made up his mind to visit the slaughterhouse in his home town of Túla while reading *The Ethics of Diet*, but he kept putting it off because of an uneasy feeling about witnessing suffering which he could not prevent. He tells of his experience in an essay called "The First Step" (*Works*, vol. 19, Colonial Press, 1905, pp. 367–409).

Tolstoy argues that there is a certain order in attaining a good life that manifests the virtue of love, which he associates with the kingdom of God. The first step is self-control and the renunciation of self-interests. It begins with that which is closest to us—our diet—and for Tolstoy this means abstinence from animal food. Tolstoy argues that killing for food is unnecessary, contrary to our moral sense, violates our deepest feelings of sympathy and compassion for all living creatures, and is provoked only by a selfish lust for "good" eating.

His depiction of a nineteenth-century Russian slaughterhouse is rather gruesome and probably not indicative of modern practices. Yet suffering is suffering, and that aspect continues. In Tolstoy's day, farmers would bring a few of their range-raised animals to town for slaughter. Today's high demand has necessitated mass producing animals and animal products by means of intensive "factory farms," which adds yet another dimension to animal suffering.

Battery hens in particular spend their lives crammed into cages which are stacked in tiers in a large dark building that reeks with urine and excretion. In a way, this reminds us of what life might have been like on Noah's ark. Imagine cramming at least two members of every animal species in the world (with fourteen of many species) into an ark that had a total deck area of two football fields. With some 20,000 species of nonaquatic vertebrates, the conditions would be rather stressful to say the least. Besides the close quarters, there would also be the smell, noise, darkness, urine and excretion accumulations, sanitary problems, as well as discomfort and frustration of the animals stacked on three decks. All of which show remarkable similarities to modern factory farms.

We could also speculate about what Noah and his family ate. Why were there so many extra clean animals (meaning fit for human consumption) on the ark? Did the extra animals only serve as food for the carnivores? Or did Noah and his family eat some of them? Was Noah's ark really an early food factory?

We have let our imaginations wander a bit, but the parallels do cause us to reflect on present-day intensive animal factories and also about the real message of the biblical story. What were all those animals doing on the ark? Why do animals play such a prominent role in the flood epic? Let us first examine the flood epic to see what we can learn, and then we will take a look at modern food factories.

Violence upon All the Earth

The pre-flood narrative in Genesis 6 depicts widespread violence throughout the earth. Both the Yahwist (6:1–8) and the Priestly (6:9–22) pre-flood stories contain statements describing the wickedness and corruption of humanity. The spread of corruption is a common experience in human history and is present in the Greek and Roman myths of the passing away of the golden age.

Of particular importance is the statement in Genesis 6:11–12 that the whole world was corrupt and filled with violence. The word for "corrupt" is the same word used in verses 13 and 17 for God's destruction of the earth. It suggests that human violence was destroying the life forms God created: humans, plants, and animals. It had reached such epidemic proportions that God had to bring judgment. Claus Westermann comments, "The earth as it should be, with the purpose for which God had created it, was destroyed" (p. 416).

In Luke 17:27 God's displeasure is perceived as partly being due to what or how people were eating: "They were eating and drinking, and marrying and being given in marriage, until the day Noah entered the ark." This suggests a link between pre-flood violence and dietary habits, which some strands of tradition explain as the unrestrained and ruthless slaughtering of animals (and perhaps humans) and gorging on their flesh. A Jewish writing dating to the second century B.C. reads, "They all corrupted their way and their ordinances, and they began to eat one another" (*Jubilees* 5.2).

The Genesis text implies that the guilt for destructive violence had spread to animals as well. The expression "all flesh" in the phrase "all flesh had corrupted its ways" (Gen 6:12) refers to all that have breath (Gen 6:17). It would appear that both animals and humans are described as savage carnivores, or at least that humans had mimicked the behavior of carnivorous animals.

The link between violence, animal abuse, and meat eating in the passage is strongly implied. Many have documented the correspondence between cruelty to animals and violent crimes, such as serial homicides. The pre-flood violence set the stage not only for the flood but also for the permission to eat meat after the flood. Louis Berman summarizes the argument of Rabbi Kook (1865–1935) by saying, "The corruption and violence which led up to the flood made it clear that because man had an insatiable desire to eat flesh, he could not yet be held to a moral standard which excluded the eating of flesh" (pp. 17–18).

The pre-flood story depicts the degeneration of humanity into a self-seeking and violent race, with extensive bloodshed and very likely unrestrained killing of animals for food. If we are correct in our reading, the story would suggest that unnecessary killing of animals simply to gorge on their flesh is part of a fallen world and is a symptom of a fallen race that has lost its moorings.

Waters upon All the Earth

There are various ancient flood stories apart from the one in Genesis, the most notable being the Gilgamesh Epic which may have influenced the biblical story. If so, the biblical traditions have transformed the material in significant ways. The reason for the flood was not to kill off the noisy humans because they were bothering the gods, as in the Gilgamesh Epic, but moral sin. In addition, the God of Israel (who is one, not many) is merciful in judgment, arranging the ark to save Noah's family and the animals.

Both the Priestly and Yahwist traditions have been woven together throughout the flood story. According to the Priestly tradition, Noah was to store enough food on board the ark for his family and the animals. Since the food was to be stored, it was presumably grain and vegetable foods. Also, the Priestly tradition (Gen 6:9–22) says that only two of every kind of animal (male and female) went aboard the ark to preserve their kind. The stored food then had to be vegetable, for to kill an animal for food would exterminate the species. Furthermore, there was no need for extra animals, since previous Priestly material forbade killing animals for food (cf. Gen 1:29–30) and the Priestly flood story does not end with a sacrifice.

However, the Yahwist story says that seven pairs of every kind of clean animal and one pair of every kind of unclean animal (e.g., carnivores) were gathered into the ark (Gen 7:1–5). There is no mention of storing food. This implies that the extra clean animals might have been food for Noah's family and the carnivores, with some being saved for Noah's sacrifice. What should we do? Should we attempt to harmonize the discrepancy in an attempt to find out what supposedly happened in back of the texts or should we accept the traditions as they stand and let God speak to us through each one?

Some have tried to harmonize the discrepancy by saying that Genesis 6 gives a general statement that at least one pair of each species was taken into the ark. Chapter 7 simply expands the details, specifying how many pairs of clean and unclean animals were to be kept alive. The larger number would then include the smaller number so that there is no contradiction.

Fine and dandy, but we quickly run into a bottleneck. Why does the Priestly tradition lack the clean/unclean distinction, lack the sacrifice at the end of the story, and have Noah stockpile veggie food? It appears that the Priestly tradition tells the story from a primeval perspective. The Yahwist tradition simply projects later clean/unclean distinctions back into primeval history. It certainly appears that we are dealing with two different perspectives on the story which have been woven together. Since both are in the Bible, we should let God speak to us through both horizons.

According to the Yahwist ending, Noah offered sacrifices to God when he left the ark (Gen 8:20–22). Noah's offering was most likely given out of gratitude to Yahweh for preserving his family through the flood. The text says that God was pleased with the smell of the sacrifice. This is a figurative way of saying that God accepts the attitude behind the sacrifice. It does not mean that God delights in the burning of flesh, the destruction of animals, or in burnt offerings. Sacrifice was simply the way people expressed themselves to God; thus God accepts it even though it is less than the divine ideal. The contrast between the biblical text and extra-biblical flood stories suggests that the word "smelling" should be taken figuratively, as we have done. Yahweh is not pictured as craving to eat the offering or swarming over it like flies as in the Gilgamesh Epic. God neither desires nor needs food to eat (cf. Ps 50:13).

God responds by pledging never again to destroy all living creatures with a flood (Gen 8:21–22). The pledge is expanded in God's covenant with Noah and every living creature (Gen 9:8–17). Both the pledge and covenant reflect a divine commitment to ensure the continuation of life, despite its having departed into violence and despite the inevitable return of violence! What we have is another "incredible God story." After revealing intense displeasure at such vile corruption, God promises to stay with us, protecting and caring for all human and animal life.

If we interpret the flood epic literally, we are immediately struck with the most extensive and ghastly slaughter of animals in the Bible—and at the hands of God, no less! Imagine the headline in *Noah's Newsletter*, "God Drowns Billions of Animals." The Israelites, however, probably did not understand the story this way. Rather they most likely viewed the flood as a symbol of God's displeasure at violence and the ark as a symbol of God's deliverance from all forms of oppression and exploitation. The hope of divine liberation is shared by all animals and humans who suffer at the hands of the oppressors, represented in the story by the violent pre-flood race. The Israelites who framed the story were forward looking people with great expectations that God would liberate them and all creation from bondage.

The story also speaks of God's love for creaturely life. Both the ark and the covenant express God's commitment to preserve human and animal life. In addition, taking every species aboard the ark tells us that God treats *all* animals kindly, whether clean or unclean, and regardless of whether humans regard them as pets or pests, wanted or unwanted, pretty or ugly, or useful or not. Furthermore, the post-flood story's ban against eating blood expresses God's desire for us to protect the sanctity of animal life against violence (to be discussed in chapter 5). As we locate our story in God's story, we too will sense God's love for all creaturely life that is conveyed by the flood story.

But did Noah actually eat some of those animals? The question is a bit misplaced, for the type of literature we are dealing with makes no pretense to answer such concerns. Nor is it of any great importance, for our faith is shaped by the narrative as we have received it rather than by what Noah supposedly ate.

The story does not at all picture the ark as a symbol of animal abuse, factory farming, or the like. Rather just the opposite is true. The story pictures the ark as a symbol of divine providence, protection, and deliverance for humans and animals alike. However, we do need to take a look at what is happening in today's factory farms and slaughterhouses. We need to listen to another set of voices. As we do, let us listen with a heart that has been shaped by the story about the ark.

Violence Once Again upon All the Earth

Violence has once again come upon all the earth, but this time God has promised not to wipe out everything. God has dramatically expressed abhorrence of killing once, and once is enough. To affirm the promise, God entered into a covenant with humanity and animals and signified it to all generations with the rainbow (Gen 9:8–17). Yet, sadly, humans have forgotten about God's displeasure at violence and have instead presumed upon God's grace—so the carnage continues.

Most people are unaware of what takes place in factory farms and slaughterhouses in order for the steak, pork chop, or fried chicken to be on their dinner plate. They rarely stop to think that the chicken or cow they are eating is a dead animal that once had feelings similar to ours and wanted nothing more than to live according to its nature. They do not realize the suffering, stress, and frustration animals undergo simply to satisfy society's inordinate desire for flesh foods. If more people were aware of the cruelty involved in producing such foods, there would be considerably fewer meat eaters, for, as Tolstoy observes, there is something deep within that says cruelty to animals is inherently wrong. Ignorance about these matters hinders our ability to make informed choices that reflect the Christian story.

The veal industry is particularly objectionable, since it is impossible to produce veal without cruelty. Veal calves are separated from their mothers at birth and spend their entire lives confined in wooden stalls. The stalls have slatted wooden floors and measure less than two feet by five feet. The narrow stall prevents them from turning around or walking. They are fed a medicated liquid formula high in protein and low in iron and are not permitted to eat roughage (i.e., grass, straw), as this would change the color of the meat. The calves consequently suffer from severe diarrhea. Nor are they permitted to romp around outside, since this would promote muscle development and produce tougher meat. Veal calves spend virtually all their lives in darkness. Lights are turned on only at meal time, and they do not see daylight until they are transported to the slaughterhouse. The only way to produce anemic animals with tender pale-colored flesh is to confine them in this extremely uncomfortable and frustrating situation.

The veal industry is an offshoot of the dairy industry. Dairy farming is profitable only if cows keep producing milk. To achieve high production, the cows are made pregnant each year and injected with hormones. When their production declines, they are shipped off to slaughter. Female calves replenish the dairy stock, while male calves are usually shipped off to veal producers. Hence, the dairy industry is implicated in the suffering of young veal calves.

The chicken industry is also rather cruel to animals. There are about 285 million hens producing commercial eggs in this country. Standard practice in egg production is to squeeze up to nine battery hens into cages measuring eighteen by twenty-four inches. Cages are then stacked in tiers so that up to 125,000 hens are housed in a single shed. Crowded conditions cause the birds stress which leads to fights, feather-pecking, and cannibalism. Since violence damages the production level, farmers resort to painful methods of debeaking. Forcing hens to produce ten times their normal egg laying production leads to acute osteoporosis, because calcium is leached from the bones to form egg shells. In addition, since egg producers are interested only in hens, they asphyxiate or grind up alive approximately 280 million male chicks each year.

Broiler production is somewhat different. Because caging causes blisters, bruises, and other injuries, broilers are not caged. Instead twenty to thirty thousand chickens are crammed into a single broiler house. Like veal calves, broilers do not see the light of day until they are taken to slaughter. Their sheds are permeated with ammonia from their droppings. Chickens raised by these methods are frightened, frustrated, in ill health, and often diseased which necessitates endless applications of antibiotics. Conditions sometimes are so bad that thousands die before slaughter. Over five billion broilers are produced each year for the American market.

One can still drive through the country and find some pigs rooting out a resting spot on the cool ground. However, most pigs today are raised intensively in crates or concrete-floored pens in narrow windowless metal buildings longer than a football field. Up to twelve thousand pigs are raised in a single building. The buildings reek with noxious fumes from such things as decaying fecal matter, ammonia, feed dust, and hydrogen sulfide.

After impregnation the breeding sow is shut in a metal gestation crate which is only a tad larger than the sow's body. For the next four months the sow remains in the crate with its concrete or metal-slatted floor with no bedding. The crates are so confining that the sow cannot walk or turn around. There are rows of such cages in a single building. Then the sow is moved to the even more restrictive farrowing crate, gives birth, allowed to nurse for an unnaturally short time, impregnated again, and taken back to the gestation crate. The cycle is repeated until the sow's production decreases, at which time she is sent to the slaughterhouse. Boars also spend their lives confined in narrow metal crates, being removed only for a short time to impregnate the sow. Young pigs are routinely sent to the slaughterhouse at about six months of age, having never seen the sun or breathed fresh air.

Pigs are intelligent, sensitive, and social animals who would normally spend their days grazing, rooting, investigating things, and socializing with other pigs. Those raised in confinement display abnormal behavior patterns (such as gnawing at the bars) which reveal emotional and psychological stress and frustration in not being able to be themselves. Factory farmed pigs must be given drugs, hormones, and antibiotics to be raised in such close and unhealthy conditions. They are treated like meat machines or production units, not like creatures with whom God has shared the joy of existence.

Peace upon All the Earth

These modern "arks" really bear no resemblance to the ark in the biblical story. The long rectangular boxes of the modern factory farm are nothing more than huge concentration camps from which the captives are taken for mass executions. In contrast to the biblical ark, these modern "arks" tell a story of bondage and death. Animals are in bondage to egocentric humans, who in turn are in bondage to their own selfish desires. Billions of animals are forced to live a miserable existence and then are needlessly slaughtered merely to satisfy our taste buds.

However, the long rectangular box of the flood epic tells a different story, a story of divine displeasure at human violence and of divine liberation from violence, oppression, exploitation, and affliction. The biblical ark functions as a prophetic symbol, pointing ahead to a time of deliverance for animals and humans alike. It illustrates the direction of the biblical narrative that leads us on the way of life toward the peaceable kingdom.

The stories of the two arks are in fact stories of the two ways. A common motif in early Christian literature is to compare the two ways of being in the world—the way of life and the way of death. The *Didache* (c. A.D. 150), for example, bases the way of life on the two love commandments (God and neighbor) and exhorts us to abstain from such things as covetousness, lying, pride, jealousy, carnal lusts, and murder. The way of death is represented by cursing, murders, adulteries, lusts, thefts, fraud, pride, malice, covetousness, and the like. For our purposes, we can contrast these two ways of being in the world as living a predatory life and living a resurrection life.

Scripture is made up of a variety of stories, many of which fall into one of these two categories. One of the most graphic biblical portrayals contrasting the two ways is the flood story. The pre-flood violence and killing, which is obviously an abomination to God, represents the way of death. It is sharply contrasted with the way of life as seen in the love, liberation, and promise symbolized by the biblical ark. A large number of stories fall between these two ways. They represent compromises and concessions in which the people of God are seen wrestling with their faith. The flood epic actually contains this third way as well, as we will see when discussing the concession to eat meat in the next chapter.

How we live in the world is contingent on what stories we identify with. Most Christians shape their identity by adopting and living several stories that ironically represent contradictory ways of being. For example, many identify with the new life of the resurrection faith but also identify with the concession to pre-flood violence; that is, they are attempting to travel down two divergent paths at the same time. It is incumbent on us, as pilgrims on the way of life, to live a consistent resurrection faith that celebrates the new life made possible by the risen Christ. How can one who is following the risen Christ any longer live a predatory lifestyle that reflects the pre-flood violence of a fallen race?

RECIPES

Meatless Loaf

1 chopped onion
2 celery stalks, diced
1 cup cooked and drained lentils

2 cups cooked millet (or cooked rice)

½ cup chopped walnuts

1 cup tomato sauce (or spaghetti sauce or canned crushed tomato)

½ cup whole wheat flour

2 cups bread crumbs (whiz pieces of whole wheat bread in blender)

½ tsp. each basil, marjoram, parsley flakes, garlic powder, cumin

1 tsp. salt

Prepare millet by cooking ½ cup dry millet in 2 cups water until water is almost absorbed; then turn off heat and let millet sit awhile to absorb remaining water. Sauté onion and celery in small amount of water and then drain. Mix all ingredients together in large bowl. Pour into an 8x8-inch baking dish and bake at 350° for 45 minutes. Serve topped with ketchup.

Pumpkin Pie

¾ cup vanilla flavored soy milk

1 29-oz. can of pumpkin

½ cup turbinado sugar (or brown sugar)

2 Tbs. cornstarch

1 Tbs. blackstrap molasses (or regular molasses)

1 Tbs. coriander

½ tsp. salt

Mix all ingredients in large bowl and pour into your favorite 9-inch pie shell. Bake at 350° for 1 hour. Let stand awhile before serving. **Variation:** Instead of the soy milk, you can substitute ⅓ cup raw sunflower seeds (or cashew pieces) thoroughly blended in ¾ cup water.

5

Didn't God Permit Us to Eat Meat?

God blessed Noah and his sons, and said to them, "Be fruitful and multiply, and fill the earth. The fear and dread of you shall rest on every animal of the earth, and on every bird of the air, on everything that creeps on the ground, and on all the fish in the sea; into your hand they are delivered. Every moving thing that lives shall be food for you; and just as I gave you the green plants, I give you everything." (Genesis 9:1–3)

If there is freedom of man to kill animals, this signifies in any case the adoption of a qualified and in some sense enhanced responsibility. If that of his lordship over the living beast is serious enough, it takes on a new gravity when he sees himself compelled to express his lordship by depriving it of its life. He obviously cannot do this except under the pressure of necessity. (Karl Barth, *Church Dogmatics* III/4, T. & T. Clark, 1961, p. 354)

Genesis 9:3 is the most significant text supporting the Christian meat-eating tradition. It presumably gives biblical and divine sanction to eat animals. William Paley, an eighteenth-century theologian, once said that if it were not for Genesis 9:3, humans would not be able to defend their "right" to eat animal flesh. Some zealous vegetarians even suggest that the verse does not belong in the Bible. However, Christian vegetarians who look to Scripture as the formative text for faith and practice would be rather averse to purging contradictory material. Our tactic therefore is a bit different. Instead of purging the text, we enter into dialogue with it. Why is the passage in the Bible? What are its historical and literary contexts? How should we view the passage in our present situation? Is it a carte blanche permission? Are there strings attached? Does God have something to say to us through this text?

How Did the Meat-Eating Verse Get in the Bible?

Something caused the Israelites to reflect theologically on their situation and to record their inspired thoughts in the Bible. Whether one opts for an early or late date of writing for Genesis, one thing is clear—animal sacrifice and meat eating had long been part of the tradition by the time of final composition. Abraham offered sacrifices to God long before Moses. The same is true about meat eating. The patriarchs were a semi-nomadic people who kept flocks and raised grains. Animals supplied them with food and other commodities, such as garments, tents, wineskins, shofars, and bone tools. After the conquest of Canaan, Israelites became an agricultural nation with more dependence on growing food from the land. Yet meat was still eaten on special occasions.

Imagine yourself as an Israelite reflecting on your traditions and experiences: "Animal sacrifice and meat eating? Well, yes, that's how everyone does it these days. But there seems to be something fishy about it." The problem for the Israelites was that animal sacrifice and meat eating played havoc with the symbols of their faith (e.g., creation peace). Tremors in one's symbolic world certainly motivate reflection, for it is what gives meaning to one's life. God was apparently accepting their sacrifices, but why? Wasn't God working toward cosmic peace as suggested in the creation stories?

It is clear that the author or editor of the early chapters of Genesis made use of previous traditions, for things are recorded that happened long before he lived. The tradition that is important to our present discussion is the Priestly tradition, which we have already encountered in earlier chapters. Priestly material addresses cultic, liturgical, and theological interests, such as sacrifice, acts of God, covenants, and divine utterances.

Those carrying on the Priestly tradition would have been acutely aware of the clash between the sacrificial system and the Genesis veggie passage, since both were part of their legacy. The meat-eating passage (Gen 9:3) is also Priestly material, which implies activity within that tradition to work out the conflict. The meat-eating passage follows and seemingly comments on the Yahwist conclusion to the flood epic in which Noah's sacrifice was accepted by God (Gen 8:20–22). Somehow the incongruity between the cosmic harmony of Genesis 1 and Noah's sacrifice (representing sacrifices in general) had to be ironed out. But, of course, the devout Israelites would not have simply made up arbitrary stories to solve their problems.

What do we do when our symbolic world clashes with our cultural traditions and experiences? The situation is rather scary, for if our symbolic world collapses, our lives become meaningless. The Israelites very likely prostrated themselves before their God. "What is God doing?" "Why hasn't God eradicated us from the face of the earth for slaughtering these beloved creatures?" "Why are we still being blessed?" They must have recognized a complexity to God's dealing with humanity that is beyond human understanding. Perhaps as they wrestled with God, they sensed God's speaking to them, the account of which passed into the oral tradition and is now preserved for us in Genesis 9:3.

The Israelites had previously understood that God forbade eating meat; now they perceive that God allows it. Has the unchanging God suddenly become capricious or fickle? To assume God cannot change would be to impose our conceptions of what constitutes deity on the ineffable and mysterious Creator. The common assumption of an immutable God is actually a Greek concept, not a Hebrew concept. The Israelites were quick to realize that they could not pigeonhole God. God is a mystery who delights in the unexpected turns of grace and love. Some ride the fence and suggest that while God's character does not change, God's relations with humanity can change. Nevertheless, the prime example of God's changing face toward humanity is God's suffering on the cross.

The Israelites therefore perceived that God was for some unknown reason condescending to the state of disorder, violence, and death in which they found themselves and that God somehow was still working among them through this inexplicable act to guide them toward the promised future. It is quite conceivable then from looking at the historical and literary contexts that the meat-eating text was due to later reflections prompted by the paradox between the Edenic visions of cosmic harmony and divine acceptance of animal sacrifice.

Command, Permission, or Concession?

When God says, "Every moving thing that lives shall be food for you," is it a command, permission, or concession? It is obvious that the statement is somehow related to the fallen state of humanity, as it is placed immediately after the fall and flood stories. It is also certain that God does not desire that we continue in the fallen state. Because of this, we should dismiss the idea that God is commanding us to eat meat. God's commands are designed to inspire us toward divine ideals, whereas God's concessions and permissions are designed to deal with us as we are. Christians traditionally have considered Genesis 9:3 as a carte blanche permission. A permission does not carry any hint of divine reservation. When the text is read as a permission, it is often projected backward into the depths of eternity in an attempt to establish that animals were intended for human use from the beginning.

Rabbinical scholars interpret Genesis 9:3 as a divine concession to the human condition or situation. The word "concession" suggests that flesh eating is something less than desirable. The difference between Jewish and Christian traditions on this passage could be due to the Christian tradition being influenced by

Aristotle and Aquinas and their idea that the lesser was created for the greater. Jewish interpreters have been more or less insulated from this hierarchical tradition. It seems best in light of the biblical narrative to regard the passage as a concession. The use of the term "concession" reminds us of God's reservations and the vegetarian ideal. It also suggests that meat eating is something less than desirable. In saying it is a concession, we part company with Aquinas and his clan and reject their teaching that animals were created primarily for human food, clothing, and the like.

Was Eating Meat God's Idea?

The narrative sequence suggests that meat eating was something humans concocted and not a divine innovation. Our meat eating passage, as noted above, comes after the stories about the fall and flood. The post-fall narrative depicts deepening corruption, violence, and killing upon the earth until God wipes out everything with the flood. The earth and its inhabitants had deviated from the path toward cosmic peace and showed no signs of repentance. We suggested in the last chapter that this violence may have included killing for food and even cannibalism. In spite of the extreme violence that filled the earth, God is merciful in judgment and arranged for the ark to save Noah's family and members of each animal species. When Noah put ashore on dry land, he offered up sacrifices in gratitude to God, sacrifices which the story has God accepting.

Then comes the concession to eat meat. The concession is part of an old tradition in Hebrew thought that sprang from illuminated reflections on how God relates to the disordered state of affairs which the story implies already included killing animals for food and sacrifice. It represents the Israelites' perception of God speaking to them in their particular situation. The Israelites must have discerned that God grants and then works through human freedom, even if that freedom results in acts which are abominable to God and which had become entrenched as social norms, such as animal sacrifice and meat eating. Rather than eradicating these customs, God starts to work through them by setting restraints to remind the Israelites of the sacredness of animal life.

The meat-eating verse occurs in a passage (partially quoted at the beginning of the chapter) that restates the dominion mandate of Genesis 1. The Israelites understood God as modifying only certain elements of the original dominion passage in light of their circumstances. Other elements remained unchanged. For example, the charge to be fruitful and multiply is retained, while the stipulation to eat only veggies is removed. An element retained from Genesis 1 that many overlook is the sacredness of human and animal life (Gen 9:4–6). What was implicit in the vegetarian passage of Genesis 1 is now made explicit. The life *(nephesh)* of the animal (symbolized by the blood) is sacred and must not be eaten for it belongs to God.

The narrative sequence does not at all suggest that God originated the idea of eating meat. The Israelites sensed that God graciously stays with them and works through their customs, choices, and wanderings to lead them onward. God still values creation and is still guiding it toward its appointed destiny. In view of the cosmic hope reflected in the Edenic narrative, it would appear that the Israelites viewed the concession to eat meat as a temporary measure and that God would wean them away from it at some future time.

What Have Others Said?

The meat-eating passage has provoked many interpretations. Some have suggested that meat eating was granted for times of need (as with famines) or for societies where vegetable food is sparse (as with the Eskimos). They remind us that the Bible was originally addressed to an audience that required animal food at various times in order to survive.

Some suggest that God often gives us what we want, even if it is contrary to divine ideals. It is said that such permission is given to show us the vanity of our ways. In 1 Samuel 8:5 the elders of Israel asked Samuel to appoint a king to lead the nation. This was not only contrary to God's desires, it was tantamount to rejecting God as their king. Even though Samuel warned the people about possible consequences, the people insisted on having a king. What did God do? God gave them a king. But everything Samuel had warned the people about came to pass, even God's not answering them in their distress.

Others suggest that the reason for permitting meat eating is to reduce human length of life. Ellen G. White views the permission as a divine judgment against sinful humanity by cutting their days short with a meat-eating diet. Other Adventists argue that by limiting human life span God effectively limits the amount of evil each person is exposed to and the time evildoers have to plague society. This is perceived as an act of mercy and love, so that people would not have to suffer an intolerable length of time due to physical, emotional, and societal afflictions. However, the health effects of meat eating was hardly a concern for the Israelites.

Still others suggest that the permission to eat meat was a temporary measure to supply food after the flood. It is argued that the flood would have destroyed plant life and thus eliminated the possibility of living on a vegetable diet. Yet Noah did not leave the ark until three months after the dove returned with a freshly picked olive leaf. There would have been plenty of vegetation to sustain Noah's family by the time they left the ark. Moreover, the herbivores survived quite well after the flood. If there was enough vegetation to sustain them, surely there would have been enough to sustain a human family of eight persons. Nevertheless, the main problem with this view is that it assumes too much from the story.

The explanation for the concession is most likely rooted in the historical and literary setting, as discussed in the opening sections of this chapter, and perhaps augmented by the first two alternate reasons given above. As one Jewish Rabbi says, the concession was "a reluctant permission." The passage does not in any way imply that eating meat is desirable. It simply allows the practice to take place within certain parameters.

Are There Any Strings Attached?

Immediately following the concession is the prohibition, "Only, you shall not eat flesh with its life, that is, its blood" (Gen 9:4). Does this mean that one is to drain all the blood from the animal before eating it? The Jews certainly interpreted it this way. Some claim that it is impossible to drain out all the blood and therefore conclude that the passage must be forbidding flesh eating altogether. This, however, contradicts the preceding verse.

The Jews were right, but there is more to it. Blood symbolizes life, and in Israelite understanding, life belongs to and is under the jurisdiction of God. Before eating an animal, the Israelites symbolically gave the life back to God by pouring the blood on the ground (Deut 12:24). The ban against eating blood therefore functions as a constant reminder that animals belong to God and are to be treated accordingly. As such, animal life is sacred and has inherent value, even though this creates a paradox with the concession to eat meat.

The Hebrew word for "life" ("you shall not eat flesh with its *life*") is *nephesh*, which refers to the animating principle in living creatures. We encountered the word in chapter 2 when discussing the creation narratives. Blood was considered to be or at least to represent the life principle *(nephesh)*. It was probably regarded as the essence of life because when the pulse stopped the animal or human had died. The Israelites adopted this symbol to express the sacredness of animated life that God had impressed upon them.

The Levitical codes specify that the blood was to be poured out beside the altar when the animal was sacrificed. This again suggests that animal life (symbolized by the blood) is sacred, not profane; and it belongs to God, not to humans. Because animal life belongs to God, humans are forbidden to treat animals any way they wish or wantonly kill them. In other words, as long as animals have the breath of life, we are to treat them kindly, with compassion, and consideration, just as the divine owner would. Animal life is not a trivial matter. It is a matter of great concern, especially to God.

The ban implies that the life of an animal is not under absolute human jurisdiction and was not handed over to such absolutism by the "dominion" passage in Genesis 1 or by its restatement in Genesis 9. Humans do have authority over creation—but it is a delegated authority to care for animals as God would and not to destroy them. All life still belongs to the Creator of life, as it did in the beginning. Old Testament scholar Gerhard von Rad observes, "Even when man slaughters and kills, he is to know that he is touching something, which, because it is life, is in a special manner God's property; and as a sign of this he is to keep his hands off the blood" (*Genesis*, Westminster, 1961, p. 128).

To summarize, part of God's original intent for creation has been temporarily modified in the concession to eat meat, but the original intent to respect and care for animals remains unchanged. The prohibition against eating blood, which represents the life of the animal, is a prohibition against mistreating God's creatures. Wanton and brutal killing of animals is totally inconsistent with a proper understanding of dominion and with its restatement in Genesis 9. The Israelites perceived that God was already working through their freedom and calling them to a more noble way of life.

Reflections for Today

What we have is a story within a story. Our canon is a collection of diverse stories, teachings, sagas, poetry, symbols, rituals, and the like, which in spite of its diversity has an inherent unity. For example, the story about God's conceding meat eating and animal sacrifice is rather diverse from the story of Eden. Yet there is a common thread, for in our text the Israelites were grappling with how to relate certain symbols of their faith with their experiences. Those symbols pertained to their hope of creation peace, justice, and liberation—symbols that are replicated in various ways throughout Scripture. The commonality of core symbols allows us to construct an overarching narrative that has a general orientation. Thus despite its diversity, the canon can still function as a formative text for faith and practice.

How then does God speak to us today through the meat-eating passage? First, we learn that God is a God of mysterious grace who deals with us as we are, not as we should be; and in a world as it is, not as it is intended to be. In other words, God gives us freedom to make our own way through life and then works through our freedom rather than eradicating it. Second, we learn that our chosen path often creates paradoxes and anomalies in our symbolic world that cry out for resolution (such as between the sanctity of animal life and killing animals for food). Third, we learn that meat eating is a concession, and being a concession it points to a more noble way of life. The concession is actually an example of a divinely inspired contextual ethic. It speaks to a particular situation, a situation which in one sense is still with us (e.g., human violence, famine, and disobedience) but which in another sense belongs to a past era (e.g., animal sacrifices).

Then what do we do? Relish in the divine concession and gorge ourselves without restraint on fried chicken and barbecued ribs? No, abusing divine grace would be totally disrespectful to God. Our lives are to be shaped by the biblical narrative, but this does not mean that we take everything slavishly literally. First, a close reading of the text suggests that the concession to eat meat is a contextualized reflection on the Israelites' situation. That is, it is culturally specific. It was God's Word to the Israelites in their situation. What we seek is God's Word to us in our situation.

Second, we recognize a very clear directional marker in the text that rises above the particular situation and contributes to the orientation of the overall narrative. God's ban against eating blood reminds us about the sacredness of animal life and points us in the direction God desires us to go. That is, it rises above the culturally specific concession to eat meat and guides us toward the promised future.

Third, as we seek the significance of the passage for today, we must let God speak to us through the text in our present situation just as God spoke to the Israelites in their situation. This means we must consider our present context. We live at a time when animal sacrifice is no longer the accepted means to relate to God, when there is an abundance of vegetable foods, and when it is possible to drop food supplies from aircraft to famine stricken areas. We also live at a time when there is an increasing outcry against animal abuse, factory farming, animal experimentation, and the fur industry.

Finally, we must remember that directional markers in the story are only guidelines. They are not to be reduced to absolute laws, otherwise the killing of animals would have to be forbidden for any reason. The text is a prime example of God's granting us freedom to trek our way through life, yet all the while urging us to a higher and more noble way of life. Our responsibility is to sense God's leading and to be faithful to the story. As we participate in the story, we will find that our attitudes and dispositions toward animals will start to change.

RECIPES

Minestrone Soup

> 2 cups bean broth (from cooking dried beans)
> 6 cups water
> 1 chopped onion
> 2 diced carrots
> 2 diced potatoes
> 2 cups cooked kidney beans
> 1 8-oz. can tomato sauce
> ½ tsp. each Italian seasoning, garlic powder
> 1 bay leaf
> ½ cup frozen peas
> 2 cups shredded spinach, chard, or other greens
> ½ cup small whole wheat shells
> 1½ tsp. salt (or salt to taste)

Boil onion, carrots, and potatoes in bean broth and water in large soup kettle until somewhat tender. Add beans, tomato sauce, and seasonings and simmer for 1½ hours. Then add frozen peas, greens, and shells. Cook another ¼ to ½ hour. Salt to taste and serve.

Hummus

> 1 cup cooked and drained garbanzo beans
> ¼ cup sesame seeds or tahini
> ¼ cup lemon juice
> 3 medium garlic cloves
> ½ tsp. salt
> ½ tsp. onion powder
> ½ cup water or bean juice

Blend all ingredients until smooth and creamy. Great on whole wheat bread, graham crackers, and pita bread.

6

Isn't Passover Lamb the Main Entrée?

They shall eat the lamb that same night; they shall eat it roasted over the fire with unleavened bread and bitter herbs. Do not eat any of it raw or boiled in water, but roasted over the fire, with its head, legs, and inner organs. You shall let none of it remain until the morning; anything that remains until the morning you shall burn. This is how you shall eat it: your loins girded, your sandals on your feet, and your staff in your hand; and you shall eat it hurriedly. It is the passover of the Lord. (Exodus 12:8–11)

Man is already on his way to homicide if he sins in the killing of animals, if he murders an animal. He must not murder an animal. He can only kill it, knowing that it does not belong to him but to God, and that in killing it he surrenders it to God in order to receive it back from Him as something he needs and desires. The killing of animals in obedience is possible only as a deeply reverential act of repentance, gratitude and praise on the part of the forgiven sinner in face of the One who is the Creator and Lord of man and beast. (Karl Barth, *Church Dogmatics*, III/4, T. & T. Clark, 1961, p. 355)

The Passover story is a curious affair. After eating the lamb, the Israelites smeared the blood on their door posts. When the death angel came to kill every firstborn person and animal in Egypt, it would pass over households that had blood on their door posts. But why all the carnage? Why are hordes of bloody, dead animals offered up to God as an atonement for sin in the Bible? To be quite honest, it is a rather repulsive thought. For many, animal sacrifice is a blight on the sacredness of Scripture and something that must be expurgated from the text. How could a God who created and loves all creatures possibly mandate and then find pleasure in the killing of animals?

The New Testament is not exempt from this criticism, for the early Christians regarded the death of Jesus as a Passover sacrifice. Do we have a sadistic God who takes pleasure in inflicting pain and suffering on animals and even on the divine son? Is God guilty of child abuse?

The notion of a sadistic God would certainly solve the problem of evil, but it hardly represents the God of the Bible. Nor can we solve the problem by expurgating objectionable material from the text. The corpus of sacrificial material is too large to casually dismiss. But this does not mean that we have to allow the sacrificial material to shape our attitudes toward animals. We must always engage the text in a careful reading in light of its historical setting, so that God can speak afresh to us today through its message.

The Paradox in a Nutshell

The difficulty with animal sacrifice is that it contradicts our perception of God's character and design for creation. If God is a God of love and compassion, then how could God possibly sanction animal sacrifice? Since animal sacrifice involves the destruction of life, one wonders how it could ever have been accepted by the Creator of life. It also appears hopelessly out of sync with the direction of the biblical narrative and the Judeo-Christian hope of creation peace. Perhaps the classic treatment of this ambiguity is *Guide for the Perplexed* by the Jewish philosopher Moses Maimonides (1135–1204). Maimonides speaks disparagingly about animal sacrifice, arguing that it was never God's highest desire for humans.

Animal sacrifice also contradicts the focus on animal compassion in the Hebrew Scriptures. The Israelites perceived that God wanted them to treat animals kindly, as indicated by the numerous laws in the Torah. But they also perceived that God was accepting animal sacrifice and allowing them to eat the meat. This has caused problems not only for our Jewish friends throughout their history but also for Christians who seek biblical grounds for animal rights or vegetarianism, unless there is a way to reinterpret the symbols.

Did God Order Sacrifices?

The first sacrifices in the Bible predate Mosaic legislation. This raises a few questions. Why did Abel sacrifice an animal to God? Why was Noah's first response to God after the flood a sacrifice of thanksgiving? Why did Abraham build altars to the Lord in the land of Canaan? Was this a normal human response or was it something God commanded?

Archaeological expeditions have found evidence of sacrificial rituals throughout the Fertile Crescent long before the Israelites entered Canaan. In pagan cultures, sacrifice was often a means to manipulate the gods, either to invoke divine blessing or to appease divine wrath. Some observe that in the ancient world animal sacrifice was as common a form of worship as hymns and prayers are today.

Since sacrifice was endemic to ancient humanity, many conclude that the Israelites simply adopted it as the normal way to express themselves to God. Yehezkel Kaufmann notes that sacrifices "were part of Israel's legacy from paganism" (*The Religion of Israel*, Allen & Unwin, 1960, p. 110). In the process of borrowing, however, the Israelites dramatically transformed the meaning of the ritual. Israel's sacrificial system was unique; it was not done as a magical enchantment to entreat the gods, win their favors, expel demons, or to accompany prayers and supplications for health and prosperity. Nor was it done to provide food for the gods. Instead, Israel's sacrificial system involved reconciliation with

God and atonement for sin. Israel may have borrowed the rite, but infused that rite with ideology quite different from pagan counterparts.

Israelite rituals in themselves did not vary much from Canaanite rituals. This is particularly evident when comparing them with the sacrifices of Baal (1 Kings 18; cf. 1 Kings 11:8; 2 Kings 5:17). Canaanite offerings consisted of holocausts (whole burnt offerings), cereal offerings, and incense offerings. One notable difference is that Canaanite rituals did not seem to attach any significance to the animal's blood.

The blood ritual is unique to Israel's sacrificial system, as is the reverence for life it symbolized. No human sacrifices were permitted. When a sacrifice was eaten, neither the blood nor fat could be consumed. The blood was to be returned to God since it symbolized the gift of life. The fat was often deemed the most savorous part of the animal, and devouring it suggested an unrestrained appetite for flesh. Hence it was not to be eaten, but returned to God. All this underscores the reverence for life that God wanted maintained while working out the divine plan through human customs with which the people were familiar.

There are several biblical texts that deny a divine origin of sacrifice. For example, Isaiah says that the people's worship of God was a "human commandment" (Isa 29:13). Jeremiah has God saying, "I did not speak to them or command them concerning burnt offerings and sacrifice" (Jer 7:22; cf. Amos 5:25). These passages support the idea that sacrifices were of human origin and that God had other notions of what constituted true religion.

Sacrifice for the Israelites was a meaningful way to worship and commune with God. In order for worship and communion to be meaningful, God had to be encountered through forms with which people could identify, such as their own language, customs, and experiences. The Israelites regarded sacrifice as a means by which their sin and guilt could be absolved and they could meet God.

In summary, it is very likely that animal sacrifice was of human origin and that it was never understood to be the divine ideal. God merely accepted an established mode of worship as a concession to human expression in order to relate to the Israelites. God's object was to wean humanity away from the practice of sacrifice by pointing to its fulfillment in the sacrifice of Christ and to other forms of sacrifice, such as the sacrifice of praise (Ps 50:12–14; Heb 13:15; cf. Jonah 2:9).

Was God against Sacrifices?

A common ploy in much of the popular literature about Christianity and vegetarianism is to argue that both God and Jesus were against animal sacrifice and were thus pro-vegetarian. Granted, there appears to be a flat-out contradiction between God's commanding sacrifices in the Torah (e.g., Exod 12:1–7) and God's displeasure with sacrifices in the prophets (e.g., Isa 1:11). Do we have a whimsical God? Are the earlier passages due to scribal corruption, as some have conjectured? How should we understand the prophetic denouncements?

Many passages suggest that God is not pleased with sacrifices. Typical is Jeremiah 6:20, "Your burnt offerings are not acceptable, nor are your sacrifices pleasing to me." Most of the passages reveal that God desires holiness and faithfulness more than ritualistic sacrifice. For example, Samuel asks Saul, "Has the Lord as great delight in burnt offerings and sacrifices, as in obeying the voice of the Lord? Surely, to obey is better than sacrifice, and to heed than the fat of rams" (1 Sam 15:22; cf. Ps 40:6–8; Prov 21:3; Hos 6:6; Micah 6:6–8). The problem was not animal sacrifice, but an unfaithful and disobedient attitude that reduced sacrifice to a meaningless ritual and a presumptuous offering for sin that lacked any significance for the worshiper. This is clearly stated in Isaiah 1:13 (NIV) where God says, "Stop bringing meaningless offerings!" As in most other denouncement texts, Isaiah continues by rebuking the people for their wickedness (Isa 1:16–23).

God also rejected other forms of meaningless worship. This underscores the idea that the issue was not animal sacrifice, but Israel's perverse attitude. In Isaiah 1:15 God does not want to listen to their prayers any longer, and in Amos 5:21–24 God will not accept their music of praise, as it is nothing but noise. The reason

God does not accept Israel's prayers, praises, or sacrifices is not because God is against these forms of worship, but because these forms of worship have been reduced to empty rituals, devoid of meaning.

God desires inward transformation of character rather than mere outward conformity to ritualistic observances. Outward forms are meaningless, unless they are practiced with corresponding inward devotion. Roland de Vaux comments,

> The Prophets condemned formalism in worship; Jeremias preached a religion of the heart; Ezekiel demanded sublime holiness; and all the most authentic spokesmen of Judaism repeat the message down to the age when the community of Qumran set before its members an ideal of piety, of penance and of moral purity. All these witnesses contributed to make the cult more interior and more spiritual; the cult was more and more considered as the outward expression of interior dispositions, and it was the inward spirit which gave it all its value. The way was thus prepared for the New Testament. (*Ancient Israel: Its Life and Institutions*, McGraw-Hill, 1961, p. 456)

It also appears that the people had turned animal sacrifice into a pretext to slaughter animals and eat their flesh (cf. 1 Sam 2:12–17; Hosea 8:13). The hypocrisy of the people is especially revealed by their eating the flesh of whole burnt offerings, which were supposed to be given entirely to God (Jer 7:21–24). Clement of Alexandria even remarks, "I believe sacrifices were invented by men to be a pretext for eating flesh" (*Stromata* 7.6). Isaiah comments that there is no atonement for those who needlessly and irresponsibly slaughter animals merely to gorge on their flesh, for doing so was considered an unforgivable sin. "There is joy and revelry, slaughtering of cattle and killing of sheep, eating of meat and drinking of wine. . . . The Lord Almighty has revealed this in my hearing: 'Till your dying day this sin will not be atoned for,' says the Lord, the Lord Almighty" (Isa 22:13–14 NIV).

Trito-Isaiah continues the long tradition of prophetic indictments against empty formalism in worship with the fiercest denouncement in Scripture. "Whoever slaughters an ox is like one who kills a human being; whoever sacrifices a lamb, like one who breaks a dog's neck; whoever presents a grain offering, like one who offers swine's blood; whoever makes a memorial offering of frankincense, like one who blesses an idol" (Isa 66:3). Reducing the divinely accepted institution to a meaningless ritual turns it into murder. This highlights the gravity of needlessly killing animals.

What the prophets condemned therefore was Israel's hypocritical formalism which was empty of meaning and void of moral commitment (cf. Isa 29:13), not the ritual itself. The prophetic denouncements imply that within the Israelite culture sacrificing animals was not wrong if done with a worshipful heart. It became wrong (and tantamount to murder) only when done without meaning and therefore needlessly. The prophets clearly were doing virtue ethics, where one's inner dispositions determine whether an action is right or wrong in any given situation.

Was Jesus against Sacrifices?

The gospel writers twice record Jesus quoting Hosea 6:6, "I desire mercy, not sacrifice" (Matt 9:13, 12:7). They also have Jesus saying that loving God and neighbor "is more important than all burnt offerings and sacrifices" (Mark 12:33 NIV). Do these statements mean that Jesus loathed animal sacrifices because it involved killing animals? Some seem to think it does. After all, Jesus is the epitome of godliness. Throughout his ministry Jesus was engrossed in preserving life and healing the infirm. How could the Jesus proclaimed by the early church as the "word of life" (1 John 1:1) possibly advocate the destruction of life?

But Jesus never called for the abolition of the sacrificial system. As a good Jewish person of the first century, Jesus respected the sacrificial system as a divinely accepted institution. He advised lepers whom he had cleansed to go to the Temple and offer the appropriate sacrifice (Mark 1:44; cf. Matt 5:23–24). Granted, there is no indication that either Jesus or his disciples themselves practiced animal sacrifice. This, however, does not mean that they thought the ritual was evil in design.

What Jesus opposed as he quoted Hosea was the abuse of the ritual, the corruption of the priesthood, and the empty formality with which sacrifices were practiced. Accordingly, Jesus stands in the line of prophetic tradition by continuing the moral protest against hypocritical formalism. Jesus confronts this abuse by driving the animal mongers and money changers out of the Temple (Mark 11:15–17; John 2:13–16). Virtually all commentators agree that Jesus' actions were directed against the dishonesty of the money changers and/or the commercialization of a holy ritual, not against the ritual itself. It was not, as some suggest, that Jesus opposed animal sacrifices and had entered the Temple to free animals destined to be slaughtered.

God had to condescend to human modes of expression, which unavoidably were less than ideal, to convey the notion of divine forgiveness. Sacrifice is then to be understood as a contextualized form of revelation (as all revelation must be). Seen in this way, God's allowing animal sacrifice was a temporary accommodation to human modes of expression until it was abolished with the sacrifice of Christ. It was never God's desire for animals to be slain.

Eating the Passover Lamb

Many types of sacrifices involved eating the flesh of the animal. Whole burnt offerings were given entirely to God and not eaten; shared offerings were partially given to God and partially eaten. It would appear from Leviticus 17:3–4 that the only time an Israelite could eat meat is in connection with sacrifice and that killing an animal solely for food was forbidden.

> If anyone of the house of Israel slaughters an ox or a lamb or a goat in the camp, or slaughters it outside the camp, and does not bring it to the entrance of the tent of meeting, to present it as an offering to the Lord before the tabernacle of the Lord, he shall be held guilty of bloodshed.

This text, which represents an early Priestly tradition, indicates that the killing of animals was originally regarded as a sacrificial act in which the animal's life was first to be given back to Yahweh. Only then could it be eaten. This means that animal slaughter had to take place at one of the various altars located throughout the land. Thus it would appear that the Priestly intent of the concession to eat meat in Genesis 9:3 would have been to allow it only in connection with sacrifice. However, with Josiah's reform and the centralization of sacrificial worship, the local altars were no longer allowed.

To alleviate the problem of obtaining meat, the later Deuteronomic tradition mitigated the Priestly restrictions. The twofold repetition of the concession in Deuteronomy states that the Israelites could kill animals for food apart from the sacrificial ritual: "You may slaughter your animals in any of your towns and eat as much of the meat as you want" (Deut 12:15 NIV). But even then the context indicates that killing was a solemn occasion and was to be done with compassion for the life of the animal.

Deuteronomy 12:20 literally reads, "When the Lord your God shall enlarge your border, as he promised you, and you shall say, 'I am going to eat flesh,' because your soul craves to eat flesh, you may eat flesh, according to all the lusts of your soul." This passage suggests that the Israelites looked upon the "permission" to eat meat as a concession to humanity's carnal desires. Rabbi Kook notes that there is an implicit reprimand in the passage (Berman, p. 94, n. 3). It reminds us of God's sending quail in the wilderness—God gave the people what they desired even though it was not God's ideal for them.

The Sacrifice to End All Sacrifices

While it is dubious to speculate whether Jesus viewed his death as a sacrifice, it is certain that the early church did. The church held that Jesus' death was the only acceptable sacrifice and the end of all sacrifices. The author of Hebrews remarks that animal sacrifices never did remove sin and that they have been superseded by the all-sufficient sacrifice of Christ (Heb 10:1–18). In the course of the discussion, the author mentions that God neither desired nor was pleased with the cultic provisions of the sacrificial system. This passage is significant because the context does not concern empty formalism, as with the prophetic denouncements, but concerns the ineffectiveness of animal sacrifices to atone for sin.

The death of Christ is foundational to Christianity. There are various interpretations of Christ's death which can be biblically supported and can convey important insights, such as the moral influence theory of Peter Abelard, the victory theory of Gustaf Aulén, and the satisfaction theory of Anselm. Nevertheless, it is difficult to disregard the New Testament reflections on Christ's death being a sacrifice. God did not originate the idea of sacrifices and we suspect was never entirely pleased with it. However, through the cross God continued to deal with humanity in ways which the people of that day could identify with and understand.

Christ's death could not be ordinary, but tragic, public, and illustrative of forgiveness. It had to be able to be interpreted as sacrifice for sin corresponding to Hebrew understanding. The cross then is a necessary form of contextualized revelation that allows humans to recognize divine forgiveness and to experience freedom from shame and guilt. It may be that God does not demand satisfaction for offending divine holiness or transgressing the law as much as God gives us freedom to cooperate in restoring relations by removing guilt. Christ's sacrifice reveals a forgiving and loving God who actively seeks reconciliation and solidarity with humanity and who calls us to a meaningful response.

Where Do We Go from Here?

In agreement with Maimonides, I would conclude that God never desired animal sacrifices. God allowed the Israelites to worship using established customs and modes of expression which were meaningful to them. It became morally wrong only when corrupted by human vices. An indifferent and disobedient attitude reduced meaningful sacrifice to meaningless murder. This strongly implies that the inspired Hebrew prophets perceived that meaningless and needless killing of animals is an abomination in the sight of God.

But the story about sacrifices does not end there. New Testament writers regularly speak of Christ's death in terms of sacrifice, but it was the sacrifice to end all sacrifices. Through the offering of Christ, God has weaned humanity away from the barbaric to more noble and uplifting forms of worship. How God could tolerate sacrifice in the first place is really beyond us. It points to the mysterious grace of God in dealing with wayward humanity as we are and on the path we have chosen.

The story about sacrifices teaches us that God grants and then works through human freedom. We have seen that God granted the Israelites freedom in worship and then worked through it, leading them to a higher form of worship in spirit and truth. In the same way God has granted freedom in diet and is now working through it, leading us to a more compassionate way of living that reflects God's aim for creation. Yes, there is freedom. But along with the freedom is the responsibility to discern where God is heading and to follow along. As we follow along, our dispositions and attitudes will be shaped in such a way as to help bring healing to our troubled society and liberation to our oppressed friends.

RECIPES

Haystacks Unlimited

> *Base:* corn chips, cooked flat noodles, cooked rice, or croutons
>
> *Second layer:* cooked dry beans (pinto, kidney, or black bean)
>
> *Third layer:* steamed vegetables (broccoli, etc.)
>
> *Fourth layer:* shredded lettuce, chopped tomatoes, and diced onions
>
> *Fifth layer:* top with Sunflower Sour Cream (chapter 1) or "Cheese" Sauce (chapter 2)

To serve, spread the base over a plate and then start building the layers into a mound or "haystack." This is an easy, tasty, and fun dish.

No-Meat Balls

¼ cup millet
1 cup water
1 cup bread crumbs (whiz pieces of whole wheat bread in
   blender)
½ cup each whole wheat flour and ground walnuts (or
   pecans)
2 Tbs. each nutritional yeast flakes, ketchup
½ tsp. each basil, marjoram, parsley flakes, onion powder,
   garlic powder
¼ tsp. salt

Cook millet in water until water is absorbed. Mix together with rest of ingredients and mash together. Form into ¾ to 1-inch balls, place on oiled cookie sheet, and bake at 325° for 30 minutes. Use with spaghetti, stroganoff, goulash, or stews.

7

Was Jesus Kosher?

[Jesus] said to them, "Then do you also fail to understand? Do you not see that whatever goes into a person from outside cannot defile, since it enters, not the heart but the stomach, and goes out into the sewer?" (Thus he declared all foods clean.) (Mark 7:18–19)

Is not the swine's flesh unclean? By no means, when it is received with thanksgiving . . . nor is anything else. It is your unthankful disposition to God that is unclean. (Chrysostom, *Homilies on Timothy* 12)

Being a good Jew, Jesus would be expected to be kosher. However, Jesus made a few radical comments that might cause us to wonder. While Jesus himself probably did not munch on pork chops (that would be too offensive), he most likely had no objection against others doing so.

We sometimes say, "That's not kosher," meaning that something is not quite proper. The word "kosher" comes from the Hebrew word *kashruth* which means "correctness" or "appropriateness." It pertains to any ceremonial or ritual practice that is acceptable by Jewish standards, whether in the selection and preparation of food, the observance of holy days, or the way in which animals were prepared for sacrifice. The roots of kosher observance are grounded in the Hebrew Scriptures, but have been elaborated on through rabbinic laws and evolving local customs over the years. During the time of Jesus, the Jews were enmeshed with their observance of biblical and rabbinic laws. Understanding the social context into which Jesus entered and the issues he was dealing with will help us understand why Jesus never condemned eating animal flesh.

Discrimination against Pigs?

Dietary laws in the Hebrew Scriptures pertain primarily to the selecting and preparing of animals and animal products to be eaten. According to Leviticus 11 and Deuteronomy 14:1–21, Israelites were allowed to eat animals, but only those classified as clean. The clean animals are divided into four groups. (a) Quadrupeds which have split hoofs and also chew the cud, such as cows and sheep, are clean and could be eaten. Those which either have split hoofs or chew the cud but not both (i.e., have a mixture), such as pigs and rabbits, are unclean and could not be eaten. (b) Water creatures with both fins and scales are clean and could be eaten. Shellfish and crustaceans would be unclean and could not be eaten, as would be eels and whales. (c) All birds are clean and could be eaten except predatory and scavenger birds, such as eagles, vultures, falcons, ravens, owls, or those that live in swamps and marshes. (d) The only flying insects that were clean were the various kinds of locust, such as crickets, katydids, and grasshoppers. Certain portions of clean animals are also forbidden, such as blood, fat, and sinew of the thigh (Gen 32:32).

The preparation of kosher foods is again rooted in Scripture but greatly elaborated on in rabbinic literature dating from the ninth century A.D. through the high Middle Ages. For example, the prohibition against boiling a kid in its mother's milk (Exod 23:19) has led to a complete separation of meat and dairy products in cooking and eating. The prohibition against eating blood has led to the custom of drawing blood out by salting, broiling, and soaking. The prohibition against eating a clean animal that dies of itself (Deut 14:21) along with exhortations in the Torah about animal compassion has led to eating only those animals which have been ritually slaughtered with a virtually instantaneous and painless death. Any signs of disease also disqualifies the animal from being eaten.

Healthy or Holy?

The dietary laws are part of a larger system of purity and impurity. God's people were to maintain purity as a reflection of the holiness of God. Appeal is often made to the holiness of God as the basis for the food laws, for example, "You shall not defile yourselves with them [unclean animals], and so become unclean. For I am the Lord your God; sanctify yourselves therefore, and be holy, for I am holy" (Lev 11:43–44; cf. Exod 22:31; Deut 14:21).

The Bible never tells us *why* some animals were clean and others unclean; it only tells us how to distinguish them. Many believe that unclean animals are dangerous to one's health, since they are mostly scavengers (pigs, shellfish) or predators that feed upon flesh (lions, hawks). But then why did Jesus and Paul abrogate the laws? Don't they care about people's health? Others argue that animals used in heathen sacrifices or thought to be deity were pronounced unclean. But then why are bulls classified as clean when they were used in sacrificial rites by Canaanites and Egyptians? It may be that the clean/unclean distinction developed over centuries and was due to several reasons: some animals may have been forbidden because of hygienic reasons (birds of prey), others because they were carnivores (lions), used in pagan rituals (pigs), evoked revulsion (snakes), or were exotic. However, there is no indisputable evidence to support these speculations.

All we can say with certainty is that the Israelites perceived that the dietary laws somehow imparted holiness which enabled them to maintain covenant relations with a holy God. The laws reminded them to separate from all forms of evil, impurity, brokenness, and mixtures, and to affirm the good, pure, and whole (cf. Lev 15:31). Through their dietary laws, the Israelites were embodying God's narrative of holistic redemption, perhaps as much as possible in their social context.

Jesus, the Radical Reformer

The gospels portray Jesus as a rather progressive Jew who said a few things that questioned the continuing validity of the dietary laws. He remarks, "There is nothing outside a person that by going in can defile, but the things that come out are what defile" (Mark 7:15). Jesus notes that food simply passes into the stomach and then is expelled into the latrine. What makes a person unclean before God are the evil thoughts which come from the heart (Mark 7:17–23).

Jesus' radical maneuver was to shift ethics, holiness, and spirituality from external rituals to inward dispositions. It was a shift from a rule-based ethic to a virtue-based ethic. Jesus was opposing the empty formalism and hypocrisy of the Pharisees, not the dietary laws per se, for it was their dispositions that rendered them clean or unclean before God, not the rituals. In other words, Jesus is telling the Pharisees, "If you want to continue your rituals—fine; just be aware that it is not the observance of these ceremonies that render you holy before God." The Pharisees had placed greater emphasis on their own traditions and rituals than on true devotion to God.

Although Jesus was focusing on inner attitudes, Mark catches the import and makes an editorial comment, "Thus he declared all foods clean" (Mark 7:19). Mark may have been influenced by Jesus' frequent violations of the ritualistic purity laws by doing such things as touching lepers (Mark 1:40–42) and dead people (Mark 5:41). By shifting purity from externals to internals, Jesus indirectly abrogates the need for ritualistic holiness based on the distinction between clean and unclean meat. This means that eating pork does not render one any less acceptable to God than eating beef. The legitimacy of eating meat is presumed.

The New Testament follows Jesus' teaching in abrogating the dietary laws and declaring that all animal foods are permissible. From a New Testament perspective, there is no reason for the

dietary laws to continue after the cross. First, the focus of the New
Covenant is on inward purity issuing from the heart rather than
outward purity based on observing rituals (Heb 8:7–13). The qual-
itatively new element in the covenant is that people will have an
inner moral capacity to live a holy life and relate to God without
the need for external rules and rituals. Holiness in the New
Testament is therefore something that flows from a changed
heart.

Second, the New Testament interprets Israelite rituals as symbols which have been fulfilled in Christ. The author of Hebrews
remarks that the rituals "deal only with food and drink and various baptisms, regulations for the body imposed until the time
comes to set things right" (Heb 9:10). Paul says, "Do not let anyone judge you by what you eat or drink. . . . These are a shadow
of the things that were to come; the reality, however, is found in
Christ" (Col 2:16–17 NIV; cf. Heb 10:1).

By rejecting ritual holiness and affirming inward holiness, the
New Testament indirectly declares that all foods are clean.
Although there are some foods that are not healthy and should be
avoided, there is no food that renders a person ritually unclean
before God. The New Testament concept of inward holiness does
have a present-day application to what one eats. We now have a
wider choice of food and a greater responsibility to choose those
things which are healthy for ourselves and our planet, embody
God's redemptive narrative, and aid us in our spirituality and
devotion to God.

The Kosher Compromise

Regulations concerning preparation of kosher foods stem from
rabbinic laws about preparing animals for sacrifice. Such laws
attempted to resolve the ambiguity between biblical texts con-
doning sacrifice and flesh eating and texts regarding animal compassion and creation harmony. The Jewish laws strike a compromise between these two conflicting themes. As we listen to these
diverse texts and the Jewish response, we hear the struggles and
perplexities of a people trying to make sense of the symbols of

their faith in light of their particular social location. The only way
the Jews knew to relate to God was through sacrifice, which God
seemingly accepted, but then this clashed with their inspired
reflections about animal compassion.

According to Jewish tradition, it is morally wrong to abuse animals or cause them pain. The mandate *tsa'ar ba'alei chayim* states:
"It is forbidden, according to the law of the Torah, to inflict pain
upon any living creature. On the contrary, it is our duty to relieve
the pain of any creature" (*Jewish Vegetarians Newsletter,* Fall 1992,
p. 11). Richard Schwartz comments, "In Judaism, one who is
cruel to animals cannot be regarded as a righteous individual" (p.
15). This is based on Proverbs 12:10 which says that righteous
people are concerned for the needs of their animals, whereas
wicked people treat their animals with cruelty. In Jewish thought
it is clearly immoral to mistreat animals; rather, one is to show
kindness toward animals and respect for their lives. When an animal's life had to be taken, it was not to be done with callousness
or brutality but with compassion and sympathy.

These attitudes influenced how animals were prepared for sacrifice, attitudes which have been passed down to us today through
the kosher laws. The Jewish method of killing is in sharp contrast
with the brutality of modern slaughterhouses. The Jewish
Talmudic laws (called *shechitah*) require the killing to be as painless and humane as possible. After the Temple was destroyed and
sacrifices stopped, the rabbis assigned the duties of animal
slaughter to certain pious persons who were thoroughly trained to
continue the humane methods laid out in the *shechitah.* The person (called *shochet*) "must recite a blessing prior to slaughter as a
reminder that he must have reverence for the life that he takes"
(Schwartz, p. 21). The kosher laws of post-Temple Judaism then
are a compromise between respect for animals and permission to
eat them.

Christianity has lost much of the compassion and kindness
toward animals preserved through the kosher laws. This is partly
due to its being influenced by Western thought. Christianity has
been bewitched by Aristotle and Aquinas' hierarchical view of animals and by Descartes' notion that animals are mere automata

that do not suffer. This tradition maintains that animals lack souls, are not objects of salvation, exist only for the sake of humanity, and that humans have no moral obligation to alleviate animal suffering.

Another reason that Jewish kindness and compassion toward animals did not readily pass over into Christianity is because of the finality of Christ's sacrifice. This meant that the Talmudic laws about humanely preparing sacrificial animals were no longer relevant. Yet, concern for animals is intrinsic to the Christian message, for Christ's death ended the need for sacrifice, and Christ's resurrection promises peace and justice for all God's creatures.

God's Love for Animals

Jewish concern for animals is patterned after God's concern. God loves animals (Ps 145:17 NIV), has compassion for them (Ps 145:9), is good to them (Ps 145:9), preserves them (Ps 36:6), provides for them (Ps 104:10–14; cf. Matt 6:26), satisfies their desires (Ps 145:16), and is concerned for their well-being (Jonah 4:11; cf. Matt 10:29).

In Ezekiel 34:1–6 God rebukes the shepherds of Israel because they are only concerned with themselves and have harshly ruled the flock. God does not rebuke them for using animals for clothing and food, but for mistreating them in the process. While the historical context pertains to the rulers of Israel, the message reverberates down to our day and rebukes anyone who mistreats those under their care, whether human or nonhuman. Perhaps God's warning in Habakkuk 2:17 is germane to our society's treatment of animals, "Your destruction of animals will terrify you" (NIV).

God's concern for animals is also seen in the covenants. The Noachian Covenant represents a divine commitment to ensure the continuation of animal life (Gen 9:8–17). The covenant, however, did not protect animals against human abuse. Hosea speaks of a future covenant that guarantees animals safety from abuse or killing (Hos 2:18).

Divine concern and love for animals are models or pointers that give orientation to our journey. We are to image God, love what God loves, and pattern our dominion after God's dominion. True Christian love reflects God's love in showing charity and compassion for all, regardless of whether they are deserving, able to return the love, or even whether they are humans or animals.

Does the Bible Really Say That?

It might come as a shock to many Christians to find out how much the Bible has to say about compassionate treatment of animals. Many assume that since God gave humans dominion over animals and lifted the restriction against eating animal flesh all moral obligations for humane treatment of animals have also been suspended. This is hardly the case. The focus on kindness and compassion toward animals throughout the Bible causes us to question such modern-day practices as animal factories, animal experimentation, the fur industry, and even the meat-centered diet in vegetable rich countries like America.

The following summary of laws in the Torah regarding kind treatment of animals comes from various traditions that have passed through centuries of animal sacrifice and meat eating. Nevertheless, animals were still to be shown compassion and consideration, even when their services were needed or their lives were to be taken for food or clothing. The following summary can function for us as directional markers to orientate us on our journey.

First, the Torah encourages us to spare animals grief. The threefold exhortation against boiling a kid in its mother's milk falls into this category (Exod 23:19, 34:26; Deut 14:21). One is not to cause grief to the mother by killing her offspring in her presence. This would show complete lack of respect for the mother-kid relation. Another command says that the calf is not to be separated from its mother for at least a week (Lev 22:27). This concern to spare animals grief is lacking in the modern veal industry where calves are separated from the mother shortly after birth.

Second, the Torah bids us to alleviate animal suffering. One is to help a neighbor's animal which has fallen on the road (Deut 22:4) and even an enemy's animal which has fallen down under a heavy burden (Exod 23:5). Jesus applies it to animals which have fallen into a ditch or well (Matt 12:11; Luke 14:5).

Third, the Torah advises us against causing unnecessary hardship to animals. The injunction about not plowing with an ox and donkey yoked together probably was made in regard to the hardship it would cause both animals (Deut 22:10).

Fourth, the Torah cautions us against inflicting unnecessary pain on animals. Balaam was reprimanded for beating his donkey (Num 22:32), and the descendants of Simeon and Levi were reprimanded for hamstringing oxen as they pleased (Gen 49:6–7).

Fifth, the Torah directs us to feed and care for animals. Exodus 23:11 commands us to provide even for wild animals. Examples of the patriarchs providing food, water, and shelter for their animals abound in the Pentateuch (cf. Gen 24:32, 33:13).

Sixth, the Torah encourages us to respect the need for animals to rest. Animals have the right to rest on the Sabbath day (Exod 20:8–10, 23:12; Deut 5:12–14). Including animals in the Sabbath regulations indicates their solidarity with humans in the creation community and that God desires that they rest from their labors just as humans do.

Seventh, the Torah urges us to respect the natural desires of animals. The prohibition against muzzling an ox as it threshes grain was given on account of the well-being and natural desires of the animal (Deut 25:4). Imagine yourself out picking strawberries on a warm day and not being tempted to pop one into your mouth. Animals have the same desire to eat as we do.

These laws challenge the commonly accepted paradigm that humans are the center around which everything on earth revolves. The biblical narrative reminds us that there are other centers that deserve respect. Simone Weil says that true love means "to empty ourselves of our false divinity, to deny ourselves, to give up being the center of the world . . . , [and] to discern that all points in the world are equally centers and that the true center is outside the world" (*Waiting for God*, Harper & Row, 1951, pp. 159–60). Even the meat-eater Solomon remarked that righteous people care for the needs of their animals (Prov 12:10). This literally reads, "have regard for the life *(nephesh)* of their animals." It has reference to being concerned for the anxieties, desires, fears, thoughts, and needs of animals.

Do Animals Suffer?

The Bible assumes that animals feel pain; otherwise, the injunctions to help animals in distress would be meaningless. One of the clearest statements that animals feel pain and suffer is Romans 8:22, "We know that the whole creation has been groaning in labor pains until now." Animals long to escape the pain and suffering in this life just as humans do. Since there is already so much suffering in the world, it would be the height of insensitivity and cruelty to inflict additional and unnecessary suffering on any living creature, whether animals or humans.

While most Christians would acknowledge that animals suffer, they do not seem to be greatly bothered by it as long as it does not take place before their eyes. It would appear that by placing animals outside the realms of salvation and moral obligation they have also removed them from the commonality of being that issues in empathy. This parallels the general consensus in our culture which may have arisen from Descartes' view of animals. Building on the notion that animals lack souls, Descartes taught that animals are mere automata, devoid of consciousness, reason, *and the ability to suffer.* The creation story, however, suggests that humans have moral obligations toward animals due to their possessing *nephesh* (the principle of animated life which includes feeling and emotion).

Animals do have feelings and can suffer pain and fear, as any pet owner can testify. The Bible is rather clear on the matter of suffering. When judgment comes upon the land and the grain supplies run out, cattle moan and flocks of sheep suffer (Joel 1:18). Animals also suffer from fear the same as humans do (Gen 9:2; Ps 104:29; Joel 2:22). Jesus has invited us to enter a story of resurrection hope for the oppressed and suffering of the world. As we live the story, our transformed lives will be a constant protest against a society that condones unnecessary animal suffering and killing.

Beyond the Kosher Compromise

The kosher laws guarded against unrestrained animal consumption and abuse by reminding the people of the sacredness of animal life and of the need to care for animals with compassion. As such, the kosher laws constitute an accepted compromise between the ideal and the permitted which enabled one to be ritually holy before God in an unholy world. It was a way for the Jewish people to make their symbolic world meaningful in their particular context. And it was into this world of kosher holiness that Jesus entered.

Jesus, however, in preaching kingdom ethics and thereby eliminating the need for holiness laws upset the symbolic world of his culture and sought to move us beyond compromise: "Be perfect, therefore, as your heavenly Father is perfect" (Matt 5:48). By locating holiness in the heart, one is able to reflect the perfect holiness of God. Jesus' teaching was designed to lead people back to the intended meaning of the Torah. Hence, kingdom ethics was not to be grounded in outward rituals and, we could add, was not to settle for compromises or concessions which sprang from the rituals. Yet most of Jesus' followers, being free from Mosaic laws and ritual holiness, fell back on the permitted rather than pressing on toward the kingdom.

Jesus' teachings have now become part of our symbolic world which we are struggling to make sense out of in light of our present context. Or said another way, they have become part of our canon within which bounds we work out our identity. How can we train the virtues and live a kingdom life in a world that tolerates oppression, exploitation, and killing? Would it not be to live at variance with a society that so casually puts up with death? Would it not be to live the story into which Jesus has invited us? The story teaches us that God never desired animals to be killed for food or sacrifice and that God permitted such practices only as concessions to human freedom and modes of expression. The story is replete with pleas about the humane treatment of animals and envisions a time when animals will be free from human abuse. Christians are called to be faithful to this story and to journey with God on the path toward peace and justice for all creation.

RECIPES

Bean Burritos

> 1 package large flour tortillas (about 10)
> 3 cups cooked, drained, and mashed pinto beans
> ¼ tsp. each paprika, cumin, garlic powder, salt
> 1 cup cooked brown rice
> 1 chopped tomato
> 1 cup shredded lettuce
> 1 bunch chopped green onions
> Your favorite Mexican sauce (taco, salsa, picante)

Drain and mash pinto beans, along with the spices and some Mexican sauce; then mix rice in with the beans. Soften tortillas by warming one at time in dry frying pan. Spread about ⅓ cup bean mixture along center horizontal line of each tortilla, adding some tomatoes, lettuce, onions, and sauce. Tuck in each end of the tortilla and then roll from bottom to top to form burrito. Place in baking dish (seam side down) and heat at 325° for 15 minutes. **Variations:** Could add chopped green peppers, sliced olives, "Cheese" Sauce (chapter 2), or Sunflower Sour Cream (chapter 1).

Vegetable Rice Pilaf

> 1 cup long grain brown rice
> 2¾ cups water
> 1 chopped medium onion
> 1 diced carrot
> 1 diced stalk celery
> ½ cup frozen baby limas

¼ cup raisins

1 Tbs. soy sauce

½ tsp. each salt and powdered garlic

(1) Prepare the onion, carrot, and celery. (2) Bring water to boil in 3-quart pot. (3) Lightly toast the DRY rice in a large DRY frying pan over medium heat, stirring constantly until the kernels pop and give off an aroma. (4) Carefully spoon toasted rice into the boiling water. (5) Add the rest of the ingredients. (6) Cover, bring back to boil, and then cook for 45 minutes at slow heat, checking after 30 minutes to see if more water is needed. This makes a tasty and fluffy rice dish. Can serve plain or with a sauce or gravy.

8

Didn't John the Baptist Snack on Locusts?

Now John wore clothing of camel's hair with a leather belt around his waist, and his food was locusts and wild honey. (Matthew 3:4)

What is a charitable heart? It is a heart which is burning with charity for the whole of creation, for men, for the birds, for the beasts, for the demons—for all creatures. He who has such a heart cannot see or call to mind a creature without his eyes becoming filled with tears by reason of the immense compassion which seizes his heart; a heart which is softened and can no longer bear to see or learn from others of any suffering, even the smallest pain, being inflicted upon a creature. This is why such a man never ceases to pray also for the animals. (St. Isaac the Syrian, cited in Vladimir Lossky, The Mystical Theology of the Eastern Church, St. Vladimir's Seminary Press, 1976, p. 111)

Many popular books on Christianity and vegetarianism claim that John the Baptist, Matthew, Peter, James, and the other apostles were vegetarians. The reason for this is rather simple. If it can be established that the early followers of Jesus were vegetarian, it would support the claim that their teacher was also vegetarian. Moreover, it would support the hypothesis that later Christians, such as Paul, departed from the vegetarian gospel of the earliest church. The assumption behind this entire line of thinking is that Christians today must base their lives on what Jesus "actually" did, rather than on the faith portraits of Jesus in the gospels and on the direction of the biblical narrative. Thus the quest to find the historical apostles goes hand in hand with the quest to find the historical Jesus.

However, as we discussed in chapter 1, it is a misguided assumption to ground Christian faith and practice in historical reconstructions rather than Scripture. Such efforts are misdirected on several accounts. First, Christian identity has always been shaped by the biblical narrative, not by historical reconstructions. The reason is that Christians are followers of the risen Christ of whom the Scriptures give testimony, not a reconstructed Jesus. This cautions us against seeking God's voice and direction for today through the endless array of dubious reconstructions.

Second, the premise that faith must be historically grounded in such a way as to pass the litmus test of certainty is a product of Enlightenment rationality. The grand achievement of the Enlightenment was to convince everyone (religious and nonreligious) that there is but one approach to truth. Accordingly Enlightenment rationality has affected both liberal and conservative Christianity. Liberals with their historical-critical method seek to find the text behind the text; and conservatives with their rational apologetics and strict correspondence theory of truth seek to anchor Christian faith in the historical inerrancy of the Bible. This is not to say that the Christian faith does not have historical underpinnings, but the problem is that both factions have responded to the Enlightenment challenge by using Enlightenment conceptual models which have then crept into their respective theologies.

Third, comprehensive, certain, and accurate historical reconstructions are simply impossible. Problems for historical reconstruction fall into two categories: (1) the historian and (2) the data or material with which the historian must work. The historian is plagued by having to be selective, needing to interpret the data, using imagination in the reconstruction of cause-effect relations, and being prone to subjectivity and biases. The historical data is plagued by being vastly incomplete, sometimes being forged or emended, often containing fictitious elements, being subject to textual corruption if preserved at all, frequently devoid of needed chronological links, and based on the selectivity, biases, and faulty memory of those recording it. Thus historical research produces a very restricted and dubious picture of past realities. The most one can hope for is a relative degree of probability.

Nevertheless, we need to take an honest look at the arguments for John the Baptist and the apostles being vegetarian to see if there is anything of substance. If they were indeed vegetarian, then understanding the reasons for their dietary choice could be beneficial for us on our journey. But to investigate the matter with the premise that their actions are somehow normative for our actions is rather misguided.

Carob Pods or Locusts?

Those who contend that John the Baptist was a vegetarian use an array of arguments. First, some argue that the "locusts" *(akris)* mentioned in Matthew 3:4 and Mark 1:6 were carob pods, not grasshoppers. This interpretation was widespread in the nineteenth century but has now fallen out of favor. The notion that it means "carob pods" (or St. John's bread) is not supported by linguistic evidence. The standard contemporary Greek-English lexicons of the New Testament define *akris* as locusts. The Greeks used another word for carob pods: *keration* (Luke 15:16). Locusts were permissible food according to Jewish dietary laws and are still commonly eaten by indigenous peoples in the Near East.

Second, the fragmentary *Gospel of the Ebionites* is often alluded to which says that John's food was "wild honey, the taste of which was that of manna, as a cake [*egkris*] dipped in oil" (Epiphanius, *Panarion* 30.13.4). The canonical gospels say nothing about a cake. Instead of *egkris* (pancake, fritter), the canonical gospels have the similar appearing *akris* (grasshopper, locust).

The question is whether the *Gospel of the Ebionites* represents a pre-Synoptic tradition or whether it was a deliberate alteration of Synoptic material. It would be more reasonable to expect "grasshopper" to be changed into "cake" than vice versa, since no one objects to eating cakes, but some would object to eating animal food. *The Gospel of the Ebionites* was probably composed around the middle of the second century, for it appears to be a harmony of the gospels (which were common at that time), and its first mention in the fathers was about A.D. 175. Modern scholarly opinion, based on literary criticism and linguistics, concludes that the Ebionites changed the reference from locusts to cakes to make John a vegetarian in order to legitimize their vegetarian beliefs.

Third, there are two references in the later Slavonic Josephus material which say that John the Baptist was a vegetarian. One insertion reads, "Every beast he abhorred (for food); . . . and fruits of the trees served him for (his) needs" (cf. *Josephus,* Loeb Classical Library, 3:645, 648). The Slavonic version is thought by some to be dependent on an Aramaic original of Josephus' *Jewish War.* However, there are no existing fragments of an Aramaic version and no evidence that the Slavonic version is based on it. Lexical analysis suggests that its underlying text is a Greek original and that the vegetarian texts are later interpolations. These interpolations and especially those of the *Gospel of the Ebionites* show that there were vegetarian sects at work in the early centuries of the church altering manuscripts to make them conform to their beliefs. Manuscripts that were in the possession of such groups should therefore be questioned.

Fourth, it has been argued by many that John the Baptist was either an Essene or greatly influenced by them and that the Essenes were vegetarian. Of all the New Testament characters, John is the most likely person to have had direct contact with the Qumran community, which according to most scholars was an Essene settlement. John's parents lived in the hill country of Judea (Luke 1:39–40), possibly near the Qumran community alongside the Dead Sea. They were quite advanced in age when John was born (Luke 1:18). If John was still a child when his parents died, the possibility exists that he was adopted by the Qumran community and raised according to their traditions. Josephus tells us that many Essenes were celibate and adopted the children of others (*War* 2.8.2).

There are several similarities between John and the Qumranites, such as being understood as the harbinger of the Messiah according to Isaiah 40:3, requiring baptism as a symbol of inward repentance and cleansing, separating themselves from the priestly Temple cult at Jerusalem, having similar eschatological expectations, and living in the same area. John's ministry centered in the southern regions of the Jordan Valley, just a few miles north of Qumran. In his travels John undoubtedly encountered members of the sect and may have visited the community, but the proximity does not demand identification of John as an Essene, and some of the parallels could be due to a common Judaistic background.

The idea that John was a vegetarian because he was an Essene cannot be established with any certainty. First, it is questionable whether John was an Essene or a member of the Qumran sect. Among the reasons against John's being an Essene are: (a) Josephus, who discusses both John and the Essenes in some detail, does not call John an Essene. (b) It is unlikely that John's father Zechariah, a priest who served in the Temple at Jerusalem, would commit his son to a heterodox Jewish sect which was opposed to the Temple priests. (c) John's open missionary activity was diametrically opposed to the practices of the closed Qumran sect. (d) John baptized people once as a sign of repentance and then sent them back into the profane world. The covenanters baptized daily as part of their purity rites in order to maintain a holy community fit for the coming Messiah.

But not all Essenes conformed to the "pattern." Josephus often speaks of Essene prophets who suddenly appeared and criticized kings. In view of such statements Otto Betz remarks, "I believe that John grew up as an Essene, probably in the desert settlement at Qumran. Then he heard a special call of God; he became independent of the community—perhaps even more than the Essene prophets described by Josephus" ("Was John the Baptist an Essene?" in *Understanding the Dead Sea Scrolls*, Random House, 1992, p. 213). Nevertheless, the most we can say with any certainty is that John probably knew of the community and interacted with them.

Second, even if John was an Essene, modern scholarship does not support the hypothesis that the Essenes were vegetarian. Section 12 of the *Damascus Document* says that fish and locusts may be eaten if prepared according to the rule. Some scholars suggest that the *Damascus Document* gives instructions for Essenes in towns and villages, whereas the *Manual of Discipline* gives instructions for those at Qumran. Nevertheless, caches of animal bones along with pot sherds have been found at Qumran which suggest that the Qumranites may have eaten meat at least on festive occasions. The bones all come from "clean" animals, and some are charred. If there is a dietary similarity between John and the Qumranites, it would be in their simple fare, not in a supposed vegetarianism. We conclude that while there was probably interaction between John and the Qumranites, one cannot prove that John was an Essene or that the Essenes were vegetarian.

Vegetarian Fishermen?

One would assume that James, Peter, and John, being fishermen, ate fish or at least were not adverse to others eating fish. Fish was a staple item for people living near the Sea of Galilee. Some suggest that the disciples became vegetarian as a result of being influenced by Jesus. This is highly questionable, for there is no convincing evidence that Jesus was vegetarian. In Luke 10:8 Jesus tells his disciples to eat whatever is set before them. Since he said this in Gentile country, he probably would have been referring to "unclean" meat. It is reasonably certain that some early Christians were vegetarians. Paul makes it clear in 1 Corinthians 8 and Romans 14 that some refused to eat meat that had been sacrificed to idols and even abstained from meat altogether as a precautionary measure. Their vegetarianism, however, would have been conditional, being contingent on their particular social location.

Eusebius preserves sections of an earlier church historian named Hegesippus (d. c. A.D. 180) who said that James, the Lord's brother, did not drink wine, eat flesh, cut his hair, or take a bath (*Ecclesiastical History* 2.23.5). Since Hegesippus was more of a traveler who wandered about collecting traditions and stories than a critical historian, his work, *Memoirs*, should be received with caution. Apparently, the source of Hegesippus's account was an Ebionite *Acts of the Apostles* which survives as fragments incorporated into the Pseudo-Clementine literature. The figure of James had special appeal to gnostic groups as the transmitter of a purer (secret) form of Christianity. It seems plausible that stories about James' asceticism may have originated from such groups. If James was an ascetic, it would suggest that he abstained from meat for spiritual reasons, not because he opposed the killing of animals.

In a context condemning gluttony Clement of Alexandria mentions that Matthew "partook of seeds, and nuts, and vegetables, without flesh" (*The Instructor* 2.1). This comment is preceded with the statement, "Happiness is found in the practice of virtue." Clement evidently used a tradition about Matthew to illustrate the virtue of self-constraint as opposed to the vice of gluttony. Without collaborating evidence, there is no way to test the validity of that tradition.

The third-century *Acts of Thomas* (not to be confused with the *Gospel of Thomas*) depicts Thomas not only as Jesus' twin brother but also as one who continually fasts and prays, eats only bread with salt, and drinks only water (9.104). The *Acts of Thomas* describes the travels of Thomas to India and back, preaching an ascetic form of Christianity. It combines popular legend with religious propaganda to promote the radical asceticism of Syrian gnostic-Christian sects. Because of this, one cannot establish that Thomas was actually vegetarian from this document alone.

The *Recognitions of Clement* portrays Peter as a vegetarian. The *Recognitions* is part of the Pseudo-Clementine literature which originated in Syria about the middle of the third century. Hans-Joachim Schoeps, echoing the consensus of leading scholars, refers to the Pseudo-Clementine writings as "a highly undependable historical novel" (*Jewish Christianity*, Fortress, 1969, p. 17). The *Recognitions* reports Peter as saying,

> I live on bread alone, with olives, and seldom even with pot-herbs; and my dress is what you see, a tunic with a pallium: and having these, I require nothing more. This is sufficient for me, because my

mind does not regard things present, but things eternal, and therefore no present and visible thing delights me. . . . For we—that is, I and my brother Andrew—have grown up from our childhood, not only orphans, but also extremely poor, and through necessity have become used to labour, whence now also we easily bear the fatigues of our journeyings. (*Recognitions of Clement* 7.6)

The Pseudo-Clementine literature was preserved by the Ebionites, a Jewish-Christian sect, which took a liking to its Jewish legalism. Epiphanius (c. 315–403), charges that the Ebionites altered history to make Peter a vegetarian (*Panarion* 30.15.1–3). Schoeps agrees, saying that "the Ebionite ideal of vegetarianism . . . resulted in 'corrections' in the portraits of several historical figures" (p. 101). Irmscher also says that the literature was interpolated by the Ebionites "so as to authenticate their irregular teaching," thereby converting "the writing into a constituent part of a Petrine, anti-Pauline secret tradition" (Edgar Hennecke, *New Testament Apocrypha*, Westminster, 1963, 2:534).

It is noteworthy that Ebionite vegetarianism is not based on kindness to animals, but on a gnostic dualism that denounces matter as evil. Epiphanius mentions that they abstained because they believed animal flesh is defiling due to its being the product of sexual intercourse (*Panarion* 30.15.4). The same idea surfaces in gnostic Manichaeism. A reason for abstinence given in another one of the Pseudo-Clementine writings is to drive away demons (demiurges?). Demons indwell humans to appropriate their organs and fulfill their lusts for meat, alcohol, and sex—things they cannot partake of in their spiritual state (*Clementine Homilies* 9.10).

The above citations about the vegetarianism of the original followers of Jesus are interesting but hardly convincing. The major problem is with their historical accuracy, much of which has been distorted by the gnostic dualism of certain Syrian sects. The most we can say is that a few apostles might have been vegetarian for ascetic reasons, but even then we are on shaky ground. We simply do not have enough substantial evidence to determine whether they were vegetarian and if they were what their reasons may have been.

Vegetarians in the Bible

Besides the statement in Genesis 1 and the implications of Isaiah 11, there are three clear examples of vegetarianism in the Bible: (1) Paul's statement in Romans 14:2 that some eat only vegetables, (2) God's feeding the Israelites manna, and (3) Daniel's diet in Babylon. The first will be the subject of chapter 10. The later two are often cited by Adventist groups in support of vegetarianism.

For most of the forty years in the wilderness the Israelites ate the manna God supplied, even though they had sizable flocks. Evidently the flocks were not numerous enough to feed large masses of people a steady diet of meat. Six weeks after leaving Sinai the people began to lust for the abundant and succulent fruits, vegetables, and meats they had in Egypt. In response the text says that God miraculously provided manna in the morning and quail in the evening (Exod 16). It appears that manna was veggie food, for it is described as "bread," was like coriander seed, and later provoked the Israelites to murmur again for the flesh of animals. Some have explained manna naturally as the honeylike droppings of the tamerisk tree. Also quail migrate through Sinai twice a year, so it was not a regular part of their diet.

A year latter the people complained about their plain veggie diet and lusted again for flesh and other succulent foods (Num 11). God was displeased with their murmuring, but nevertheless provided what they desired by again sending quail. The people killed more than they could possibly eat and began gorging themselves, which again provoked God's wrath. This prompted God to send a plague as a rebuke for their carnality and gluttony.

The manna stopped when the Hebrews ate the grains and vegetables of Canaan. The story could be viewed as a summary of the Judeo-Christian position on meat eating. What displeased God was not their eating meat, but their inordinate desire for succulent foods and their gorging themselves. While clearly against gluttony, God allows freedom to eat meat even though it is not the ideal. God acknowledges the intensity of human desires and patiently works with us. Thus we do not find laws telling us to abstain from meat after the fall. What we find instead are exhortations to turn to God in faith and obedience and to overcome vices (such as gluttony) through the power of the Holy Spirit. This suggests that dietary reform is partially contingent on a spiritual reform. Humans will continue to crave and gorge themselves on animal flesh and other succulent foods until vices are transformed into virtues so as to be content with a simpler fare.

In contrast with the manna in the wilderness, God provided Elijah with bread and animal flesh *(basar)* twice a day by means of ravens (1 Kings 17:6). Some suggest that "ravens" should read "Arabians"; nevertheless, the provisions were said to be from God, and they included animal flesh. However, God provided Elijah with bread rather than meat before he went on a pilgrimage to a sacred place (Horeb) to receive a divine vision (1 Kings 19:5–8). Does this imply that the Israelites perceived something unholy about killing for food? Does it suggest that we should abstain from flesh before seeking God's face in worship and prayer?

A noted example of vegetarianism in the Bible is Daniel. Daniel and his friends refrained from eating the king's food and drinking his wine because they did not want to defile themselves (Dan 1:5–16). Most likely, they regarded the food as defiling because it had either been offered to pagan gods or not been prepared according to Jewish dietary laws. Instead of eating the king's meat, they ate vegetables (KJV pulse) and water.

Abstaining from Gentile food was practiced by other pious Jews of the same period in an attempt to maintain Jewish identity amid the forced hellenization by the ruling Seleucid dynasty (Tobit 1:10–13; Judith 12:2). The story of Daniel's refusing the king's meat probably served to encourage other Jews who refused pagan food, such as the pork that Antiochus Epiphanes tried to force on them.

It appears that Daniel's vegetarianism was conditional and that it stemmed from a strict observance of the dietary laws. Daniel probably would not have had any qualms about eating properly prepared meat that was not offered to pagan gods. It is questionable whether Daniel was a resolute vegetarian, since he tells of a three-week fast in which he abstained from meat before receiving a vision (Dan 10:2–3). This mantic vegetarian fast implies that at other times he did eat meat.

The Undoing of the Quest

There is no clear evidence that John the Baptist or the early apostles were vegetarian and if they were what their reasons might have been. The quest to find the historical Jesus and apostles becomes a misguided excursion into futility when it is driven by the assumption that the result would be normative for people today. The dietary practices of the early church cannot in any way be held up as normative for Christian conduct. Not only are historical reconstructions problematic, diet itself is always conditioned by one's social location and cannot be held up as a universal norm. Moreover, as mentioned before, Christians are shaped by the biblical narrative, not by historical reconstructions.

If the quest is placed within the context of gleaning thoughts from the early church to help us on our journey, then it can become a meaningful investigation. Our exploration, however, did not yield much help from the earliest apostles. It would be much more beneficial to examine the writings of the early church fathers who are replete with discussions encouraging a simple diet (often without meat) for Christians of their era. We will look at them in chapter 11. But even then it would not be that their discussions are normative for us, rather their reasons might be of some help as we make decisions for our journey.

RECIPES

Millet Burgers

> ½ cup millet
> 2 cups water
> ½ cup whole wheat flour
> 1 cup quick oats (or rolled oats)
> 1 finely chopped medium onion (uncooked)
> ¼ cup chopped walnuts
> ¼ cup ketchup, spaghetti sauce, or tomato sauce

1 Tbs. soy sauce

½ tsp. each cumin, garlic powder

Cook millet in 2 cups water until water is almost absorbed. Turn off heat and let pan sit on burner awhile to absorb rest of water. Then mix the cooked millet with the rest of the ingredients in a large bowl, using extra moisture if needed to enable patties to be formed. Form into patties with a hamburger press and bake at 350° on an oiled cookie sheet for 30 minutes. Makes 8 to 10 3-inch burgers. Serve in hamburger buns with all the trappings, or with gravy (see below), Sunflower Sour Cream (chapter 1), or "Cheese" Sauce (chapter 2). **Variations:** Try adding bread crumbs, thyme, celery seed, Italian seasoning, soy flour, yeast flakes, a shredded and stewed carrot, or up to 1 cup cooked and drained lentils, or even dry blending the oats.

Country-Style Gravy

6 Tbs. white flour (or whole wheat pastry flour)

2 cups water

1 Tbs. nutritional yeast flakes

2 tsp. onion powder

¾ tsp. salt

½ tsp. garlic powder

¼ tsp. each paprika and ground celery seed

Combine all ingredients in saucepan and cook over medium heat until thickened, stirring constantly with wire whisk. **Variations:** (1) For darker gravy, use whole wheat pastry flour, 1 tsp. black-strap molasses, and 2 Tbs. soy sauce (reducing extra salt if necessary). (2) For richer gravy, replace the flour with ½ cup cashew pieces and 2 Tbs. cornstarch and blend all ingredients in blender until smooth. Pour into saucepan and cook until thickened, stirring constantly.

9

Doesn't God Care about Our Health?

Do you not know that your body is a temple of the Holy Spirit within you, which you have from God, and that you are not your own? For you were bought with a price; therefore glorify God in your body.
(1 Corinthians 6:19–20)

Christianity does not require [abstaining from wine and animal food] . . . . I began to do this about twelve years ago. . . . But I resumed the use of them both about two years after, for the sake of some who thought I made it a point of conscience, telling them, "I will eat flesh while the world standeth", rather than "make my brother to offend". Dr. Cheyne advised me to leave them off again, assuring me, "Till you do you will never be free from fevers". And since I have taken his advice I have been free (blessed be God) from all bodily disorders.
(John Wesley, *Works*, vol. 11, Abingdon, 1989, pp. 344–45)

In 1993 I attended a HealthFest conference and heard Anne Frahm talk about how changing to a vegetarian diet played a large part in overcoming cancer. The doctors had declared her cancer to be beyond hope. Frahm, who grew up "keeping McDonald's in business," never wanted to go vegetarian. But facing death, she turned to a nutritionist who radically changed her diet. Other factors which she says contributed to her overcoming cancer include exercise, support from her family and friends, and belief in God. Her cancer has totally disappeared (cf. Anne Frahm, *A Cancer Battle Plan,* Pinon, 1992).

Similar stories are fairly common, many of which are documented by physicians, such as those Dean Ornish tells about (*Dr. Dean Ornish's Program for Reversing Heart Disease,* Ivy, 1996). Ornish comments,

> There are more and more reasons to eat a plant-based diet. More evidence is accumulating that a low-fat vegetarian diet may not only help prevent heart disease and stroke but also some of the more common cancers. . . . Vegetarians also have lower rates of osteoporosis, adult-onset diabetes, hypertension, obesity, and many other illnesses. (p. xxxi)

But if a veggie diet has such healing power, why did God allow meat eating? Does God want us all to die off with heart attacks and cancer? Or is God just letting us play a risky game of dietary roulette as we trek our own way through life?

Is Health a Christian Concern?

When was the last time you heard a sermon encouraging exercise and a healthy diet? If you're like most people, you probably have never heard such talk from the pulpit. It is ironic that the church faithfully prays for those who are sick, but hardly utters a word to encourage people to adopt a healthy lifestyle. It appears that the church is concerned about people's health only after they get sick, not before. For many the Christian faith pertains only to the spiritual aspects of life—salvation of souls, prayer, worship, and morality. This truncated view of Christianity may have resulted from the rise of the scientific world view to dominance during the Enlightenment. Instead of critically engaging the new thought and offering an interpretation of the physical world, many retreated to pietism, fideism, quietism, or a quasi-Gnosticism, leaving the physical realm in the hands of objective science.

However, the physical is very much part of the Christian life and hope. Jesus went about healing the sick, encouraging his followers to give food and water to the needy, and exhorting them to love God with all their heart, soul, mind, and strength. In addition, the biblical narrative suggests that God is at work guiding all creation to a redeemed state that is no longer plagued by human sin (cf. Rom 8:19–21). John anticipates a new heaven and earth; that is, spiritual and physical realms devoid of corruption (Rev 21:1). God's redemptive plan does not divorce the spiritual from the physical, but rather focuses on cleansing the physical from the effects of evil.

This cleansing of the physical is evident in Paul's discussion about prostitution. In 1 Corinthians 6 while exhorting his readers to shun fornication, Paul comments that it is a sin against the body itself. Paul follows with the grounds for prohibiting fornication, "Do you not know that your body is a temple of the Holy Spirit within you, which you have from God, and that you are not your own?" (1 Cor 6:19). Paul used this same pattern earlier in the book when speaking about building up the church (1 Cor 3:16–17). The difference between these two passages is that chapter 6 is speaking of the individual person while chapter 3 is speaking of the community as the dwelling place of God's Spirit.

A moral exhortation based on an indwelling deity was common in the Hellenistic world, as for example in the writing of the Stoic moralist Epictetus (*Discourses* 2.8). Whether or not Paul adopted a Hellenistic idea is somewhat beside the point, for whatever Paul did, it is clearly infused with a Christian perspective. Moreover, the passage is now part of the Christian canon that shapes Christian identity.

Our text speaks about the encroachments of evil into the physical realm, or as Paul puts it, sins against the body. It speaks of actions that disgrace or damage our bodies and thereby introduce corruption into that which is destined to be whole. Besides fornication, we might include gluttony, drug addiction, drunkenness, self-mutilation, and suicide. Some suggest that meat eating should also be regarded as a sin against the body.

Nevertheless, God can speak to us through the passage in several ways. First, our bodies belong to God, not to us. This means that we do not have the right to damage or destroy them. Rather we are to be faithful stewards of a gift which God has entrusted to our care. Second, redemption is viewed holistically. In saying, "You were bought with a price," Paul clearly includes the body in redemptive history and rejects a gnostic dualism that depreciates the body. Those who focus entirely on the salvation of souls and neglect the physical aspects of creation are guilty of espousing a gnostic dualism. Third, we are to glorify God in our bodies. Instead of using our bodies merely to gratify gastronomic and sensual cravings, we are to use our bodies to honor God by allowing the Spirit to purge corrupting elements so that they might testify of the transforming power of the risen Christ.

Could Eating Be Hazardous to Your Health?

Should we include meat eating among the sins against the body that Paul spoke about? It is rather obvious that eating flesh is damaging to the health of the animals being eaten, but is it damaging to the health of humans? It might appear that those who eat a macho diet of 16-ounce steaks are rather hefty and robust fellows. But are they gambling their lives on satisfying their taste buds? The following discussion summarizes some of the current medical research that suggests eating meat could have adverse affects on our health.

First, the high-fat, high-cholesterol, high-protein, and low-fiber content of an animal-based diet has been implicated in a variety of human diseases, such as atherosclerosis, heart disease, stroke, adult-onset diabetes, various forms of cancer, and a host of other ailments, including kidney stones, osteoporosis, and obesity. Medical science has for the most part conquered infectious diseases but is having trouble with chronic degenerative diseases, such as those mentioned above. The reason is that these diseases are primarily due to the lifestyle and diet of affluent societies. They are often called "diseases of affluence." Meat, for example, contains high levels of protein, fat, and cholesterol and is devoid of fiber and carbohydrates. To base one's diet mostly on meat is to invite trouble. It has been estimated that two-thirds of all deaths

are related to lifestyle and dietary choices. For many, this is reason enough to cut back or abstain from the consumption of animal products.

Second, many diseases in cattle and poultry (some of which
are caused by intensive animal farming methods) can be trans-
mitted to humans. Meat inspectors cannot insure that only dis-
ease-free meat is sold to the public. USDA inspectors, for instance,
must sit on the production line and examine roughly seventy
chickens per minute with what is called the "poke and sniff"
method. Also FDA plant inspectors are able to visit the 53,000
food-processing operations in this country only once every ten
years. There is no way such token inspections can protect the public. Moreover, the USDA's new monitoring plan will allow 20 percent of a plant's processed chickens to contain salmonella! Some
of the diseases in animals that might affect humans besides salmonella include campylobacter and *E. coli* bacteria, bovine
leukemia virus (BLV), bovine immunodeficiency virus (BIV),
trichinella worms, toxoplasmosis parasites, hepatitis viruses, certain cancers, as well as the ever-threatening mad cow disease.
About 9,000 people in the United States die each year from food
poisoning, of which an estimated 1,000 to 2,000 die from salmonella poisoning. The USDA reports that 70 percent of all foodborne illnesses are caused by infected meat and poultry.

The mad cow epidemic in Great Britain was due to cattle being
fed the processed carcasses of sheep that were infected with a disease called scrapie. This fatal disease, called bovine spongiform
encephalopathy (BSE), causes microscopic holes in brains. While
the FDA has banned feeding mammalian tissues to cattle, the mad
cow epidemic demonstrates that foodborne diseases can jump the
species barrier and that eating animal tissue carries a potential
risk of contracting the same disease the animal carried. The
human counterpart to BSE is called Creutzfeld-Jacob disease
(CJD), but it is still questionable whether human cases are the
result of eating infected cows (*JAMA*, Sept. 24, 1997, pp.
1008–1011).

Third, there appears to be a greater risk of chemical contamination in flesh foods than vegetable foods. The residues of antibi-

otics and hormones used on animals to combat diseases and promote growth are often present in meat. People who eat meat potentially consume harmful residues of these drugs as well as residues of the pesticides used on the feed grains. Since pesticides and herbicides are fat-soluble, they tend to accumulate in the animals' fatty tissues. In all fairness to the meat industry, we must remember that foodborne diseases and pesticide contamination are also found in vegetable foods, such as hepatitis being found on strawberries imported from Mexico. To lower the risk of pesticide contamination, we try to buy organic produce whenever possible and avoid imported fruits and vegetables. Those who eat meat, however, will find it extremely difficult to be selective consumers. Local supermarkets rarely give consumers the option to buy beef from cattle which had been raised on organic feed and without antibiotics.

If smoking, taking drugs, and meat eating could be hazardous to one's health, as many medical and nutritional experts are now suggesting, then Christians should begin questioning whether these activities best exemplify the aims and goals of the Christian hope. Richard Schwartz even comments that meat eating is a slow form of suicide, and, of course, suicide is not exactly a kingdom ideal (p. 34). Because of the rise in diseases related to high fat and high cholesterol intake, vegetarianism can be viewed as a responsible diet that reflects the Christian beliefs about our bodies being God's property and being included in God's redemption. Eating a healthy diet then becomes a spiritual exercise that expresses our symbolic world in a meaningful way and testifies of our hope in a holistic redemption with justice, peace, and healing for all creation.

Wasn't Canaan Flowing with Milk and Honey?

Why do many vegetarians exclude other animal products from their diet, such as dairy and eggs? Dairy products are mentioned throughout the Bible, the most notable of which is Canaan's being described as the "land flowing with milk and honey." The expression, however, is nothing more than a poetic description of bounty that uses the language and idiom of the Israelites. The primary reasons people abstain from dairy products and eggs are again related to ethical and health issues, to which we can add a few thoughts about the way God's creation functions.

First, health-related reasons for abstaining from milk include the possibility of its containing bovine diseases, antibiotic residues, and antibiotic-resistant bacteria. In addition, eggs and dairy products may contain salmonella bacteria. They also contain high levels of cholesterol and animal protein. Consuming large amounts of animal protein has been linked with calcium depletion from the bones. It is commonly thought that osteoporosis is due to a low calcium intake, but medical research has shown that it is due to a high intake of animal protein which leaches calcium out of the body (McDougall, *Plan*, pp. 102–3; *Program*, pp. 382–84; Barnard, pp. 18–21).

Second, dairy farming is not without questionable ethical practices, such as making cows pregnant each year to maintain milk production, separating newborn calves from their mother, confining male calves to small stalls their entire lives and denying them their natural diet in order to produce veal, injecting dairy cows with hormones to increase milk production, and sending them to slaughter when their milk production declines.

Third, we should note that the practice of drinking the milk of another species is a rarity in nature. While many humans drink cow's milk, some are allergic to it. Studies have shown that there are fundamental differences between cow's milk and human milk and consequently that cow's milk best nourishes calves, not people. For example, cow's milk contains three times the amount of calcium and phosphorous, twice the amount of protein and sodium, and half the amount of carbohydrates and iron as human milk.

Fourth, the practice of drinking milk after infancy is also a rarity in nature. The natural use of milk is to nourish newborn mammals, not adults. You may ask, "But don't we need calcium from cow's milk?" This question bothered us too until we discovered that many people do not drink milk at all, do not take calcium tablets, and still do not suffer from calcium deficiency. In rural China, for example, where vast numbers of people consume very little meat and no milk, there are virtually no cases of osteoporosis. It would appear that adults do not need milk for a source of calcium, as advertised by the milk industry.

While difficult for many to accept, it does seem that medically and ethically, abstaining from dairy products is part of the journey toward peace, justice, wholeness, and healing throughout all creation. It also seems to be in accord with the way nature operates. It is a matter not only of being stewards of our body and caring for the animals under our custody but also of being sensitive to where God is leading and wanting to be part of the resurrection procession.

Aren't Preachers Supposed to Be Fat?

Does it matter how much we eat? One glance at the stereotypical preacher reveals a rather corpulent fellow who seems to sanction gluttony as a standard Christian practice. Both biblical and early church writers were quite adamant against overindulging in food, associating it with lust, inordinate desire, carnality, and ill health. We know today that overweight people are much more prone to coronary disease, strokes, and cancer.

Gluttony means excessive eating and drinking, regardless of the kind of food. However, whenever the Bible mentions the kind of food involved with gluttony, meat is always included. It appears that overindulgence in meat is particularly offensive to God. For example, God was angered when the children of Israel gorged themselves on quail and when Eli's sons' demand their portion of meat before it was offered on the altar (1 Sam 2:12–17). Proverbs also warns us against overindulgence in meat: "Do not join those who drink too much wine or gorge themselves on meat [*basar*], for drunkards and gluttons become poor, and drowsiness clothes them in rags" (Prov 23:20–21 NIV). Proverbs 23 begins with the warning, "When you sit to dine with a ruler, note well what is before you, and put a knife to your throat if you are given to gluttony. Do not crave his delicacies, for that food is deceptive" (Prov 23:1–3 NIV).

Gluttony is not simply eating large quantities of food. It is eating more than one needs. That is, it is eating when not necessary. What is so offensive to God when gluttony involves meat is that animals have to be killed needlessly simply to satisfy peoples' gastronomic cravings. It is the unnecessary killing that provokes divine displeasure. One only wonders what God thinks about the great quantities of meat consumed in vegetable rich countries where meat eating is no longer necessary.

Gluttons are those who make their belly their god (Phil 3:19) and who live to eat rather than eat to live. Gluttony then is not only an unnecessary and unhealthy practice, it also reflects an egocentric vice to please self without regard for how it might affect others in the community of creation.

Striking a Balance

While personal health is a powerful motive for vegetarianism, it is questionable for Christians to abstain from meat purely for health reasons. The problem is that it may feed a deep-seated imbalance that has difficulty seeing past itself. This imbalance is reflected by the modern beauty, sex, and macho cult that worships the body and neglects care for others. As Christians we should be concerned with caring for all life in the creation community, rather than simply keeping ourselves fit and trim. To become obsessed with our own health and longevity rather than attending to the broader concerns of peace, love, and healing for all is symptomatic of the egocentric, narcissistic cult of a fallen race. It is as if self-worship is replacing belief in God, and the modern quest for the fountain of youth (through diet and exercise) is replacing belief in the afterlife. Even though there are dangers in overemphasizing personal health, health is still a valid Christian concern grounded in the concepts of stewardship, holistic redemption, and the Christian story.

The same criticism can be charged against Christian vegetarianism that is based solely on environmentalism or animal rights. Again, only a segment of total healing is in view. The problem is that the source for determining values and direction comes from our own fragmentary plane of existence rather than being informed by the overall direction of God's narrative. A focus on personal health would be tainted with an anthropocentric outlook, whereas a focus on environmental or animal rights issues would be tainted with a biocentric outlook. Neither is broad enough to take in the concerns of the other. The only viable perspective for a Christian is a form of theocentrism, where God's narrative is the basic source of value, meaning, and direction in life.

In addition, renewing the body must not take priority over renewing relations with the Creator. Misplaced priorities often distort something that is inherently good. Jesus warned the masses who were following him simply to be healed or fed that spiritual restoration was more needful than physical restoration (John 6:26–27). He also warned his followers that those who were intent on saving their lives would end up losing them (Matt 16:25). When we become entangled in self-interests, our spiritual balance becomes skewed, and we end up driving the wedge of separation deeper into our fragmented world.

Thus personal health is a valid Christian concern, but it cannot be the only reason for vegetarianism from a Christian viewpoint. If the broader perspective of the biblical narrative is not maintained, then vegetarianism can easily become reductionistic and cultish, with too much focus on self rather than on others in the creation community. The most coherent form of vegetarianism for Christians is "theocentric vegetarianism" that focuses on participation in God's narrative. A theocentric perspective on vegetarianism readily takes into consideration the needs of humans, animals, and the environment. We do not eliminate these concerns by centering on God; rather God encompasses them. God is working for many of the same goals celebrated in the health, vegetarian, and animal rights movements and has given us hope of their coming to pass through the risen Christ.

Expanding Our Vision

Most Christians who are vegetarians today do so for health or ethical reasons derived entirely from our present social location. The

Bible presents a seemingly insurmountable obstacle for constructing theological reasons for vegetarianism. Grounding one's vegetarianism on health reasons is an easy way to avoid the difficulties and the diverse voices in the text, but it actually compounds the problem. Why does God allow a diet that could be hazardous to our health? Why did Jesus, the perfect exemplar of human conduct, consume food that might be unhealthy? And why, if eating the flesh of animals is unhealthy, did Paul say that God created animals to be eaten (1 Tim 4:3)? Doesn't God care about our physical health?

Yes, God cares. But God also grants us freedom to make choices, even if those choices might be detrimental to our health and the health of the planet. This reflects not only a loving and gracious God in not demanding that we partake of a certain diet but also an incomprehensible risk-taking God. We freewheeling humans have certainly taken advantage of our freedom, but in so doing we have botched things up and caused massive and needless pain and suffering not only on ourselves (with cancer, heart disease, and the like) but also on innocent animals in factory farms and laboratories. Sometimes we shake our heads in bewilderment at why God allows such goings on. But God does not abandon us to our freedom. As we stumble along our ill-chosen path, God's Spirit stays with us turning tragedies into blessings and wooing us to return to the journey heading toward peace and healing throughout creation.

The Christian hope anticipates healing which is both spiritual and physical. This reflects Jesus' ministry of healing, Paul's concept of cosmic salvation, and John's vision of a new heaven and a new earth. It simply does not square with the Bible to view the Christian hope as an ethereal existence devoid of the physical. The Bible suggests that physical, social, emotional, and psychological health are integral parts of a holistic vision of salvation. Imagine what heaven would be like if everyone were in wheel chairs, receiving chemotherapy, or plugged into feeding tubes. Hopefully, heaven is not a glorified nursing home.

But is the Christian hope of healing and renewal limited to humanity? Paul makes it clear in Romans 8:18–25 that Christ's redemption pertains to the well-being of nonhuman creation as well as to humans. We don't really know how literal to take all this or what exactly it will entail, but one thing is sure. It is part of our symbolic world that molds our identity and shapes the way we think and act. That is, the vision not only represents the end of the journey, but the path itself. It represents part of what God is up to in the world and part of the business we should be about as followers of God on the journey.

RECIPES

Pasta Primavera

> 1 lb. package frozen California vegetable blend
> 4 cups whole wheat flat noodles
> 1 8-oz. can tomato sauce
> 1 Tbs. cornstarch
> ½ tsp. salt
> ½ tsp. each basil, dill weed
> ¼ tsp. garlic powder

(1) Steam vegetables until tender. (2) Cook noodles in rapidly boiling water for 12 minutes, drain. (3) Heat rest of ingredients in saucepan, stirring constantly with a wire whisk until thickened. (4) Toss all together and serve. **Variation:** In place of the frozen vegetables, could use fresh vegetables, such as a couple carrots, a potato, onion, and some broccoli.

Carob Pudding

> 1¼ cup hot cooked millet (or cooked "gummy" rice)
> ½ cup whole pitted dates (firmly packed)
> 2 Tbs. + 1 tsp. carob powder
> 2 Tbs. chopped walnuts, pecans, or 1 Tbs. peanut butter

pinch of salt
extra water

(1) To prepare millet, cook ⅜ cup dry millet in 1½ cup water until water is almost absorbed. Turn off heat and leave pan on burner awhile to absorb rest of water. (2) Cut dates into pieces to make sure pits are totally removed and then put into blender along with cooked millet and rest of ingredients. (3) Add just enough extra water to be able to blend and give good consistency, usually about ⅜ to ½ cup. (4) Blend until smooth and creamy. (5) Chill and serve.

10

Didn't Paul Condemn Vegetarianism as Heresy?

Now the Spirit speaketh expressly, that in the later times some shall depart from the faith, giving head to seducing spirits, and doctrines of devils; . . . forbidding to marry, and commanding to abstain from meats, which God has created to be received with thanksgiving of them which believe and know the truth. For every creature of God is good, and nothing to be refused, if it be received with thanksgiving: for it is sanctified by the word of God and prayer. (I Timothy 4:1–5 KJV)

The apostle reprobates likewise such as "bid to abstain from meats;" but he does so from the foresight of the Holy Spirit, precondemning already the heretics who would enjoin perpetual abstinence to the extent of destroying and despising the works of the Creator; such as I may find in the person of a Marcion, a Tatian, or a Jupiter, the Pythagorean heretic of to-day; not in the person of the Paraclete. (Tertullian, *On Fasting*, 15)

The mention of the apostle Paul in vegetarian circles invariably invokes some sarcastic and disparaging remarks. Why is this? Well, for one thing, Paul is read through the lens of modern issues. This gives the impression that he would be one of those passionate and inexorable meat eaters who could care less about animal suffering. On top of that, Paul is read through the lens of a hypothetical reconstruction which claims that he was the first to pervert the vegetarian teachings of Jesus and the earliest apostles so as to make the gospel more acceptable to his meat-eating Gentile audiences. This supposedly led to the dominance of meat eating throughout church and society today. Our text for this chapter is frequently offered in support of Paul's anti-vegetarian position.

Paul clearly stands in need of a fair shake. Hopefully, in the past chapters we have laid to rest the entire fiasco of trying to base Christian ethics on historical reconstructions. If we can clear from our minds the hypothesis that Jesus and the early apostles were vegetarian and that Paul perverted this "pure" teaching by allowing meat eating, then perhaps we can see Paul's writings on the subject in a new light and allow God to speak through them to our situation.

The Heretics' Feast

Our text for this chapter comes from the first letter to Timothy. Its authorship has traditionally been attributed to Paul. However, most scholars conclude that it was written by one of Paul's disciples who carried on his basic teachings. Developments probably occurred within the Pauline tradition that would have led to some modifications. This cautions us about categorically blaming Paul for everything we read in the Pastoral Epistles.

The text was purposely chosen from the KJV because it uses the word "meat." The word "meat" occurs some fifty-seven times in the KJV New Testament, making it appear as if it was a central part of the diet of the early church. For example, Jesus often "sat at meat"; John the Baptist advises the people to demonstrate repentance by sharing their meat with others (Luke 3:11); and the early church met together and ate meat with gladness (Acts 2:46). However, most of the Greek words underlying the KJV's "meat" are generic terms for food. The now archaic expression "sit at meat" represents a Greek word that means to recline at dinner. Thus the usage of the word "meat" in the KJV New Testament does not necessarily refer to animal flesh. When the KJV was translated, one of the meanings for "meat" was food in general.

The author says, "In the latter times some shall depart from the faith, . . . forbidding to marry, and commanding to abstain from meats" (1 Tim 4:1, 3 KJV). The word the KJV translates "meat" is *brōma*, one of the generic terms for "food" mentioned above (cf. NRSV). Commentators, however, usually interpret *brōma* in this passage in the specialized sense of "animal flesh." The reason for this is its association with abstaining from marriage. This nexus reveals that the opponents were involved in a dualistic belief system, similar to the gnostic teachings that plagued the church during the second and third centuries. It is clear that they held that physical things were evil and spiritual things were good. Thus procreation (e.g., marriage, sexual relations) or any fruit of procreation (e.g., physical bodies, animal flesh) were evil. Gnostic groups of the first several centuries regularly forbade both marriage and meat eating. We should note in passing that a similar dualistic belief was the reason for the strict vegetarianism among the Syrian gnostic-Christian sects that produced much of the literature used to "prove" Jesus and the apostles were vegetarian. Actually the beliefs the author confronts here in Ephesus appear to be a syncretism of Christianity, Judaism, and incipient Gnosticism, similar to the Colossian heresy.

One may wonder why the author was so harsh against this brand of vegetarianism (calling it doctrines of demons), whereas in Romans 14 Paul was much more cordial to another form of vegetarianism. The answer is that it was not vegetarianism per se that was under attack and regarded as heresy, but rather the debasing of God's creation. The author condemns only those who turn vegetarianism into an absolute law because they believe that the physical creation is evil. He is not condemning those who choose to abstain from meat for other reasons, such as to avoid any possibility of eating meat offered to idols (cf. Rom 14:1–6). Thus within the Pauline tradition, it would have been perfectly acceptable to abstain for the right reasons.

The author repudiates this radical asceticism, as did the early apologists, by saying, "For every creature of God is good, and nothing to be refused, if it be received with thanksgiving" (1 Tim 4:4 KJV). The word "creature" translates *ktisma*, a generic word for all that God made. The author is affirming the goodness of God's creation. Whatever God has provided for us to eat therefore is to be received with thanksgiving, for it is inherently good, having come from God's good creation. Whether or not the food is the best for one's health, had been polluted by chemicals, or raised in animal factories are contemporary issues that lie beyond the scope of the author's thought.

Ancient Error in Modern Guise

It is obvious that if God spoke to the writers of Scripture, God did so within the social location of the authors—and in our passage that social location (or context) is both similar and different from ours. We are no longer plagued by a radical dualism that denounces the physical as evil. Thus Paul's specific condemnation of vegetarianism does not apply in our context. What does apply are those elements in the story that transcend Paul's particular situation. These elements then will be the grid through which God can speak to our generation.

What we learn is that God's creation is not to be debased or devalued. In the first few centuries of the Christian era, this devaluation surfaced in dualistic religious beliefs; today it surfaces in the abusive treatment of animals in laboratories and food factories. Apart from the paradoxical pampering of pets, our society has virtually deprived animals of any value apart from research, amusement, monetary gain, or being something to eat. Animals have become mere commodities or objects to exploit with no inherent value.

While our text is culturally specific, there emerges from it a signpost that orientates us in the direction of the biblical narrative. From God's approval of creation (Gen 1:31) to God's redemption of all creation (Rom 8:19–21), we learn that the created world is good and is to be valued for its own sake. Just as the early church denounced those who devalued creation, the church today should denounce animal abuse wherever it is found, for it too debases God's good creation.

Ironic as it may seem, the devaluing of animals by the Gnostics led to a very strict vegetarianism, whereas the devaluing of animals today leads to an unrestrained eating of meat. The early church responded by condemning gnostic vegetarianism. But how do we, in the spirit of 1 Timothy 4:1–5, protest against the modern devaluation and abuse of animals in the food, medical, entertainment, and fur industries? Would not a vegetarian diet be an integral part of our protest? In summary, we should note that this passage, far from being the sore spot in vegetarian circles, is one of the clearest New Testament protests against the devaluation of God's creatures.

Touch Not; Taste Not; Handle Not

A slightly different brand of asceticism is found among the opponents Paul confronts in Colossians. In Colossians 2:16–17 Paul writes, "Do not let anyone judge you by what you eat or drink, or with regard to a religious festival, a New Moon celebration or a Sabbath day. These are a shadow of the things that were to come; the reality, however, is found in Christ" (NIV). The opponents in Colossae appear to be a syncretistic sect that had fused Jewish beliefs and rituals together with Christianity and mystical astrology, with possible elements from a mystery religion and an early form of Gnosticism.

Their ascetic dogma renouncing certain foods and drink may have been intended to aid one in gaining access to the "elemental spirits of the universe" who supposedly directed the stars, calendar, and everyday events (Col 2:20). Paul summarizes their laws in the following verse, "Touch not; taste not; handle not." It is not certain whether the prohibitions refer to gnostic abstinence from sex and flesh foods or to foods pronounced unclean by Jewish dietary standards. The adversaries, however, seem to be more stringent in their religious asceticism than the traditional Judaizers Paul dealt with in Galatians and may be akin to the later Ebionites.

Paul argues that the Jewish rituals (which here had been reworked with non-Jewish elements) were only shadows prefiguring a reality that has been fulfilled in Christ. Therefore observance of these ascetic practices and rituals is no longer necessary. Access to God is now through Christ, not through rituals or elemental spirits. Therefore Paul tells the Colossians not to let anyone condemn them in their eating habits and to ignore those who insist on abstaining from certain foods.

Whether the asceticism was due to gnostic or Jewish influence, the implication is the same—Paul saw nothing wrong with eating meat. Again, we must understand Paul within his context. If we lift the passage out of context, it makes him look like an arrogant and contemptuous meat eater who would not tolerate anyone trying to restrict his diet. Paul is not really addressing the issue of meat eating or vegetarianism, but rather the transitory status of symbols that pointed to the Messiah. We often forget that one's perception of proper and improper behavior is usually conditioned by one's social location in dialogue with one's symbolic world. The particular social locations that contributed to Paul's reflections regarding the food problems at Ephesus, Colossae, Rome, and Corinth are considerably different from our situation.

Did Paul Ever Preach Salad?

In Romans 14:1–3 Paul says, "Welcome those who are weak in faith, but not for the purpose of quarreling over opinions. Some believe in eating anything, while the weak eat only vegetables. Those who eat must not despise those who abstain, and those who abstain must not pass judgment on those who eat; for God has welcomed them." Paul is saying that if one wants to be vegetarian—fine; if one wants to eat meat—fine. Only don't let one judge the other, for each is to live in good conscience before God and with consideration for others in the community.

Paul is addressing problems confronting Jewish Christians in Rome. It would have been very difficult for Jewish Christians living in a pagan city to be sure their meat had not been offered to idols or had been prepared according to Mosaic ceremonial laws.

Therefore some chose not to eat meat at all. In Romans 14:2 Paul says they ate only vegetables *(lachanon)*. Their vegetarianism was conditional, like that of Daniel. There would have been no objection to eating meat if it was ceremonially clean according to Mosaic law and not offered to idols.

Problems arose when certain Christians (the strong) asserted that these foods were acceptable to eat, paraded their liberty before those who ate only vegetables, and ridiculed them for their narrow-mindedness. Paul, however, never legislates the "proper" diet. While he accepts the validity of eating meat per se (cf. Rom 14:14, 20), he does not condemn the weak for their position nor praise the strong for theirs. What he objects to is the weak despising the strong for their free lifestyle and the strong ridiculing the weak for their narrow-minded scruples; that is, what made their conduct objectionable was not what they ate, but their inner dispositions. It appears that, for Paul, wrongdoing in the case of diet is not determined by a prior rule, but by the outflowing of inner vices.

Paul recognizes that some believers will have stronger feelings of what is pleasing to God because of their Jewish background. He calls these "weak" because their conscience could easily be offended. It is in no way meant to be a derogatory term. Those who practiced vegetarianism were concerned about their food being properly prepared according to Jewish dietary laws. Paul had personally rejected cultic and ritual concepts of purity in favor of inward holiness. However, he saw no problem for those who held such scruples, as long as they did not condemn those who differed and did not view the practice as meritorious for salvation.

Instead of legislating the "proper" diet, Paul gives his readers the responsibility to form their own convictions on the matter in light of what they felt was proper before God. He writes, "Let all be fully convinced in their own minds" (Rom 14:5). Paul only asked that they apply the larger issues of peace, edification, and community to their particular situation; in other words, to apply the directional markers that emerge from the biblical narrative to their specific decision making process.

Paul's model for ethics appears to be more narrative and virtue based than rule based. It is a rather dubious procedure to construct a code of absolute ethics based on selected prooftexts, as they tend to be culturally specific and to be at variance with one another. Paul encourages us to let God speak through the orientation of the biblical narrative in light of our own context to make moral decisions. It would not be surprising then as we view today's abusive animal factories through the lens of the biblical narrative that we arrive at a stronger position than Paul regarding vegetarianism.

Does Freedom Have Boundaries?

The situation Paul faced in Corinth differs slightly from that in Rome. Gerd Theissen argues that those Paul calls "weak" in Corinth include lower class Jewish and Gentile Christians (*The Social Setting of Pauline Christianity*, Fortress, 1982, pp. 128–29). Greek cities had public food distributions of grain on which the lower class primarily lived. While the rich could afford meat, the common people ate meat only at public cultic rituals. Problems arose when they converted to Christianity. Being poor, it would be tempting not to miss out on free food at pagan temples; yet, being Christian, it would be difficult to partake of something offered to idols.

The issue at Corinth clearly pertained to eating meat in pagan temples. Some Corinthians believed that this practice was wrong. Their conscience was defiled whenever they participated in the temple meal. Paul responds by saying that our relation with God will not be affected whether we eat or abstain. God is indifferent about external rituals. Paul, however, advises his readers against flaunting their liberty by eating meat in a pagan temple and thereby enticing others to partake against their conscience (1 Cor 8:7–13).

In light of this, Paul tells his readers that it is permissible to buy marketplace meat, take it home, and eat; for food is a gift of God and is to be received with thanksgiving. But he cautions his readers against eating meat at the home of an unbeliever if it would offend the conscience of other guests who might question the morality of eating (1 Cor 10:25–30). Paul was always willing to limit his liberty out of respect for the sensitivities of others. He summarizes his view of Christian liberty with two very important thoughts: (1) not everything which is permitted is beneficial, and (2) one should seek the good of others rather than one's own good (1 Cor 10:23–24). When these focal images are read in light of the divine concession in Genesis 9:3 and in light of our present context, the implications are rather astounding.

Even though the situation in Corinth, like that in Rome, is culturally specific, Paul's wisdom transcends the circumstances. God has granted liberty in the eating of meat, but Paul reminds us that not everything that has been permitted is beneficial—for us or for our community. He acknowledges that eating meat can sometimes be very detrimental. In addition, we should seek the good of others in the community (and today that may mean others in the community of creation). The selfless love of Christ who gave himself for others should govern our disposition about seeking the good of others rather than our own good.

Paul's liberty then had boundaries, and those boundaries are defined by what constitutes a virtuous life in his particular context. Condemning others for their eating habits or arrogantly parading one's liberty before others stems from inner vices and would clearly be wrong. Christians have always maintained that they have liberty to eat meat, but this does not necessarily mean that there are no boundaries. The eating habits of those who devour large quantities of meat and thereby help create the need for abusive animal farms do seem to cross over an ethical boundary. These practices implicate people in the institutional vices of cruelty and callousness which pay no regard to the lives of our fellow creatures.

If one avoids the evils associated with gluttony and animal abuse, one is still left with the choice of whether to continue with eating an occasional humanely grown animal. Paul's thought encourages Christians to go all the way and totally abstain. Paul remarks that if eating animal flesh (*kreas*) causes the downfall of a fellow believer, he would totally abstain from eating meat for the rest of his life (1 Cor 8:13; cf. Rom 14:21). Even though Paul taught dietary liberty, it was not reckless liberty. As F. F. Bruce notes, "A truly emancipated spirit such as Paul's is not in bondage to its own emancipation" (*Commentary on Acts*, Eerdmans, 1954, p. 432, n. 39). Having been emancipated from bondage to the law, Paul is now free to be a slave to others. This means that he is open to become a vegetarian if necessary out of love for others in the community.

From Paul the Villain to
Paul the Liberator

If a hard-core vegetarian read Paul only through the lens of today's situation, where widespread gluttony is propelling the most inhumane industry humanity has ever devised, then he or she would probably write him off as a narrow-minded meat-devouring bigot. "Sure, go ahead and buy that meat at the market, there is nothing wrong with it." No, we must interpret Paul in light of his social context and the circumstances he was addressing. Instead of combating the evils of animal factories (which, of course, did not exist), he was trying to work through the food problems his readers faced that sprang from gnostic dualism, Jewish dietary laws, and pagan sacrifices.

Apart from the ban against eating unclean animals, the only dietary practices condemned in Scripture are cases of inordinate desire and consumption, eating with unthankful hearts, grounding a dietary habit on the debasing of animals, causing other Christians to stumble, and absolutism on the part of either vegetarians or meat eaters. All stem from wrong dispositions. Again, it is not what is eaten that is wrong, but the inner attitudes. Since the Bible leaves diet as a spiritual choice, we are encouraged to exercise discernment to determine the best course in our present context.

We have much to learn from Paul's method of decision making. In every passage discussed in this chapter, Paul applies directional markers that emerge from the overall biblical narrative to specific situations. He does not resort to prooftexting to support or denounce particular dietary practices. When we talk about "directional markers" (such as peace, renewal, community), we do not mean "principles." There is a difference. Principles are often reduced to absolute and binding rules which are concretized into a deontological (rule-based) ethic.

Directional markers, on the other hand, emerge at various places throughout the biblical narrative and function as flexible guidelines for the journey. That is, they give us a degree of freedom as well as a general orientation to make decisions as we travel toward the kingdom. The image of the kingdom in particular orientates us toward seeking peace and righteousness throughout the created order. Our task is to let God speak to us through the lens of the biblical narrative to our own situation in which animals are being debased and abused.

I would like to close this chapter with a reflection by an early church father named Origen. In responding to the antagonist Celsus, Origen said that he could not understand how abstaining from meat offered to idols means that Christians should refrain from all flesh. Nevertheless, he continued,

> We do not indeed deny that the divine word does seem to command something similar to this, when to raise us to a higher and purer life it says, "It is good neither to eat flesh, nor to drink wine, nor anything whereby thy brother stumbleth, or is offended, or is made weak;" and again, "Destroy not him with thy meat, for whom Christ died;" and again, "If meat make my brother to offend, I will eat no flesh while the world standeth, lest I make my brother to offend." (*Against Celsus,* 8.28)

R E C I P E S

Taco Salad

    2 cups cooked and drained pinto or kidney beans
    1 head lettuce, broken into bite-sized pieces
    1 diced medium onion
    4 chopped tomatoes
    1 8-oz. jar Thousand Island dressing (vegan)

> 1 16-oz. bag tortilla chips
> 1 6-oz. package shredded non-dairy cheese (optional)

Toss all together in a very large bowl. Great served as a main dish for a small group on a warm summer day.

Granola

> 1 cup pitted dates
> 1 cup juice (orange, apple, pineapple, or grape)
> 6 cups rolled oats
> ¾ to 1 cup each coconut, raw sunflower seeds, chopped
>   walnuts or pecans
> 1 Tbs. coriander
> ¾ tsp. salt
> ¼ cup soy or whole wheat flour

Cut up dates and then whiz in blender with 1 cup juice until creamy. Mix the remaining ingredients together in large bowl. Pour date mixture into the dry ingredients and stir/mash together with heavy potato masher until everything is moist and starting to clump together. Then spread out in two jelly roll pans (or cookie sheets with sides or bottoms of broiler pans). Bake at 325° for ½ hour, then at 250° for 1½ hours more. Take out at each half hour interval to stir and rotate pans between upper and lower shelves. After the 2 hours are finished turn off oven and leave granola in for awhile.

11

Is Christian Vegetarianism Only for Desert Monks?

Do you not know that in a race the runners all compete, but only one receives the prize? Run in such a way that you may win it. Athletes exercise self-control in all things; they do it to receive a perishable wreath, but we an imperishable one. (1 Corinthians 9:24–25)

The former [Pythagoreans] abstain on account of the fable about the transmigration of souls. . . . We, however, when we do abstain, do so because "we keep under our body, and bring it into subjection," and desire "to mortify our members that are upon the earth, fornication, uncleanness, inordinate affection, evil concupiscence;" and we use every effort to "mortify the deeds of the flesh." (Origen, *Against Celsus* 5.49)

The earliest form of monastic life in the early church was the solitary desert monk. Most of us probably have stereotyped impressions about what the life of a desert monk was like, such as living a rather strict Spartan-like existence secluded from society. Desert monks did discipline their body, but not because they thought it was evil. Rather they were concerned with keeping the vices (or what they called passions) from controlling their lives, for that would stand in the way of achieving the goal of selfless love to others. Their spiritual exercises frequently included abstinence from meat, strong drink, and sexuality, areas in which the passions often run wild.

Many of the early church fathers had similar views about controlling passions and cultivating virtues. They too considered meat eating morally wrong if it involved gluttony. To control the passions, the fathers recommended a simple diet for all Christians, often with vegetarianism as an option or at least abstinence from meat on certain days. For the monastics, however, abstinence became a way of life and something expected among those seeking perfection. Some held that eating meat stimulated inordinate sexual desires. Thus meat eating was not appropriate for an "athlete of Christ" (cf. 1 Cor 9:25–27).

In addition, the early fathers fought against a heretical form of vegetarianism that sprang from gnostic dualism. The gnostic belief that the physical realm was evil turned meat eating and marriage into works of the devil. Since the fathers believed the world was good, they could not condemn meat eating. The willingness to eat meat was for them a certification of orthodoxy.

Although six of the following fathers (Clement of Alexandria, Tertullian, Origen, Basil, Chrysostom, and Jerome) are sometimes set forth as examples of vegetarians in contemporary vegetarian literature, none of them insisted that their followers totally abstain from flesh foods. Whether they themselves were strict vegetarians is difficult to discern. Their writings focused on a simple diet that avoided gluttony while condemning and maintaining distance from gnostic ascetics who insisted on vegetarianism.

Clement of Alexandria (c. 150–c. 215)

To help the believer avoid being preoccupied with worldly things, Clement of Alexandria advocated a simple, plain diet to "purge the eye of the soul, and to sanctify also his flesh" (*The Instructor* 2.1). He condemned gluttonous persons who lived for the gratification of their belly. "Excess, which in all things is an evil, is very highly reprehensible in the matter of food." Instead, he recommended a moderate diet to maintain health, strength, and spiritual vigor.

"The diet which exceeds sufficiency injures a man, deteriorates his spirit, and renders his body prone to disease" (*The Instructor* 2.1).

Clement did not condemn meat eating in moderation, "We are not, then, to abstain wholly from various kinds of food, but only are not to be taken up about them." He continues, "If one partakes of them [meat and wine], he does not sin. Only let him partake temperately, not dependent on them, nor gaping after fine fare." He sets forth Jesus' multiplication of the loaves and fish as "a beautiful example of simple food" (*The Instructor* 2.1). His simple fare did lean toward quasi-vegetarianism:

> For is there not within a temperate simplicity a wholesome variety of eatables? Bulbs, olives, certain herbs, milk, cheese, fruits, all kinds of cooked food without sauces; and if flesh is wanted, let roast rather than boiled be set down. . . . But those who bend around inflammatory tables, nourishing their own diseases, are ruled by a most lickerish demon, whom I shall not blush to call the Belly-demon. . . . It is far better to be happy than to have a demon dwelling with us. (*The Instructor* 2.1)

This passage is often quoted without the reference to eating flesh, thus wrongly making it appear that Clement taught strict vegetarianism. Clement considered vegetarianism to be a spiritual choice, "If any one of the righteous does not burden his soul by the eating of flesh, he has the advantage of a rational reason, not as Pythagoras and his followers dream of the transmigration of the soul" (*Stromata* 7.6).

Tertullian (c. 155–c. 230)

Tertullian, an early Latin church father, strongly condemned gluttony and eating rich foods. "For to you your belly is god, and your lungs a temple, and your paunch a sacrificial altar, and your cook the priest, and your fragrant smell the Holy Spirit, and your condiments spiritual gifts, and your belching prophecy" (*On Fasting* 16).

When Tertullian was between forty and fifty years old, he became disenchanted with the laxity in the Roman church and was drawn to Montanism with its asceticism, holiness, and morality. Montanism was a prophetic movement, similar to the charismatic church today, but whose members practiced fasting and ate plain, dry foods (xerophagy). Xerophagy is described by Tertullian as the practice of keeping food unmoistened by any flesh, juiciness, succulent fruit, or wine (*On Fasting* 1).

Tertullian rejected xerophagy as an obligatory rule, likening it to "heathenish superstition." He argues that "faith, free in Christ, owes no abstinence from particular meats to the Jewish Law even, admitted as it has been by the apostle once for all to the whole range of the meat-market" *(On Fasting* 2). Yet, he accepted xerophagy as a choice to aid one's spirituality. In commenting on Daniel's vegetarianism Tertullian wrote, "The 'pitiable' spectacle and the humiliation of xerophagies expel fear, and attract the ears of God, and make men masters of secrets" (*On Fasting* 9).

Tertullian taught that it was contrary to Scripture to command perpetual abstinence, as done by the "Pythagorean heretics," for this would be "despising the works of the Creator" (*On Fasting* 15). In response to the radical ascetics he commented that Christians abstain only on special occasions: "For how limited is the extent of *our* 'interdiction of meats!' Two weeks of xerophagies in the year (and not the whole of these,—the Sabbaths, to wit, and the Lord's days, being excepted) we offer to God; abstaining from things we do not *reject*, but *defer*" (*On Fasting* 15).

Saint Hippolytus (c. 170–c. 236)

Hippolytus was a Greek-speaking presbyter and the most famous theologian and apologist in the church at Rome during the third century. In one of his writings he strongly denounced the dualistic asceticism of the Marcionites who considered the physical world to be void of value and intrinsically evil. To avoid evil Marcion required strict asceticism from his followers, which included abstinence from meat, wine, and sex (Hippolytus, *Refutation of All Heresies* 7.18).

One of Marcion's reasons for abstinence from meat is the possibility of eating a soul which had been punished by a demiurge.

In confronting gnostic dualism and transmigration of souls, Hippolytus and the other early apologists consistently affirmed the goodness of God's creation. Marcion was excommunicated in A.D. 144, but his teachings were quickly disseminated throughout the Roman Empire. Most of the Marcionites were absorbed into Manichaeism by the end of the third century.

Origen (c. 185–c. 254)

Origen, a disciple of Clement of Alexandria, was one of the greatest theologians and apologists of the early church. In a response to a pagan treatise attacking Christianity, Origen remarked,

> We are indeed to abstain not only from the flesh of animals, but from all other kinds of food, if we cannot partake of them without incurring evil, and the consequences of evil. For we are to avoid eating for gluttony, or for the mere gratification of the appetite, without regard to the health and sustenance of the body. (*Against Celsus* 8.30)

It appears that Origen did not see any problem with eating flesh if it did not involve inordinate desire and consumption.

In reference to eating meat, Origen commented, "We do not set great store on refraining from eating, nor yet are we induced to eat from a gluttonous appetite. And therefore, so far as we are concerned, the followers of Pythagoras, who abstain from all things that contain life, may do as they please" (*Against Celsus* 5.49). Origen notes that the Pythagoreans abstain because of their belief in the transmigration of souls, whereas Christian ascetics abstain in order to control the passions. "If we abstain at times from eating the flesh of animals, it is evidently, therefore, not for the same reason as Pythagoras" (*Against Celsus* 8.30).

Novatian (210–280)

The Roman presbyter Novatian suggested that God granted flesh to eat because of the rigors of life outside of paradise (*On the Jewish Meats* 2). He believed that humans simply needed more strength. He also suggested that some meats were withheld (dietary laws) to teach moderation in appetite (*On the Jewish Meats* 4). Like other church fathers, he argued for liberty in diet, but not luxury:

> For those things only are to be taken by which our soul may be made better; and although in the Gospel the use of meats is universally given to us, yet it is understood to be given to us only with the law of frugality and continence. For these things are even greatly becoming to the faithful,—to wit, those who are about to pray to God . . . cannot be if the mind, stupefied by meat and wine, should not prevail to shake off heavy sleep and the load heaped upon the breast. (*On the Jewish Meats* 6)

Novatian based his law of frugality and continency on 1 Timothy 6:8 where Paul stated that having food and clothing we should be content.

Saint Anthony (c. 251–356)

Anthony was one of the earliest Egyptian desert monks. He took up the ascetic life at about age eighteen and began living in a tomb at an abandoned cemetery near the Nile River. When Anthony was about thirty-five he retreated to the desert mountains and took up residence in an abandoned fort. He was well known for his virtuous life, struggles with the demons, and intercessory prayers. His asceticism could be taken as representative of other early solitary monks. In his *Life of Anthony*, Athanasius comments,

> He ate once daily, after sunset, but there were times when he received food every second and frequently every fourth day. His food was bread and salt, and for drinking he took only water. There is no reason even to speak of meat and wine, when indeed, such a thing was not found among the other zealous men. (sec. 7)

Friends would regularly bring him bread. He ate only out of necessity, so that the soul might not be "dragged down by bodily pleasures." Anthony spent much of his life at an oasis at the foot of a mountain between the Nile River and the Red Sea, which had water, date palms, and even a place to grow his own grain for bread. Later in life he partook of olives, pulse, and oil that friends brought him. Anthony died at one hundred and five years of age and was buried in the mountains by two friends (*Life of Anthony* sec. 45, 49–51, 92).

Saint Basil the Great (c. 330–379)

Basil the Great, bishop of Caesarea, was an ardent defender of Nicene Christianity. He introduced communal monasticism as an alternative to individual asceticism. The Rule of Saint Basil is based on love, holiness, obedience, and social involvement and remains as the foundation of Orthodox monasticism today. Basil advocated a simple diet for spiritual reasons:

> For a man in good health bread will suffice, and water will quench thirst; such dishes of vegetables may be added as conduce to strengthening the body for the discharge of its functions. One ought not to eat with any exhibition of savage gluttony, but in everything that concerns our pleasures to maintain moderation, quiet, and self-control; and, all through, not to let the mind forget to think of God, but to make even the nature of our food, and the constitution of the body that takes it, a ground and means for offering Him the glory, bethinking us how the various kinds of food, suitable to the needs of our bodies, are due to the provision of the great Steward of the Universe. (*Epistle* 2.6, "To Gregory")

Like other church fathers, Basil championed moderation. He did not approve of excessively gorging oneself on meats since it tended to darken the light of the spirit. He even questioned whether one can really have virtue if the appetite is allowed to run wild. But Basil also disapproved of extreme asceticism. During the third and fourth centuries monasticism flourished along with such practices as sleeping standing up, wearing hair shirts, living on top of pillars, mixing ashes with one's food, and burning one's fingers rather than give in to sexual desires. Basil was one of several fathers who sought to limit such ascetic excesses.

Saint John Chrysostom (c. 347–407)

John Chrysostom spent much of his life as an ascetic. After the rigors of asceticism in the mountains ruined his health, he returned to the city and took up the preaching for which he is best known. He argued that Christians should be kind and gentle to animals, "The souls of the Saints are very gentle and loving unto man. . . . And even to the unreasoning creatures they extend their gentleness" (*Homilies on the Epistle to the Romans* 29). His simple diet in earlier years, however, appears to be due to his asceticism rather than to the belief that animals should not be killed for food.

In his homily on 1 Timothy 4:1–3 Chrysostom condemned the Manichaeans, Encratites, Marcionites, "and the whole of their tribe" for their forbidding meat eating and marriage. He referred to these sects as seducing spirits and heretics who have departed from the faith and speak lies in hypocrisy (*Homilies on Timothy* 12).

Chrysostom condemned gluttony, not meat eating. He said, "We are not commanded to avoid dainties as if they were unclean in themselves, but as they corrupt the soul by excess." He continues by asking, "Is not the swine's flesh unclean? By no means, when it is received with thanksgiving . . . nor is anything else. It is your unthankful disposition to God that is unclean." Chrysostom affirmed that to insist that people "abstain from meats is the doctrine of devils" (*Homilies on Timothy* 12).

Chrysostom's dietary boundaries were contingent on sufficiency to support one's health. He mentions that those who can maintain good health with pulse should seek nothing more, those who are weaker may eat vegetables, and those who are even weaker "and require the support of flesh in moderation, we do not debar him from this" (*Homilies on Second Corinthians* 19.3). In another homily he harked back to his ascetic days by encouraging his listeners to be worthy of the wedding feast. As examples of those who would be considered worthy, he referred to those holy persons who live in the desert, wear garments of hair, and abstain from meat (*Homilies on the Gospel of Matthew* 69).

Saint Jerome (c. 340–420)

Jerome is known not only for translating the Greek and Hebrew Scriptures into Latin but also for his kindness toward animals.

Stories even have him befriending a lion. Jerome, however, did not advocate vegetarianism because he believed killing of animals was morally wrong. Instead he recommended a diet of vegetables, fruit, and grain for Christian people because it was easier on the digestive system, was easier to prepare, would aid one's mental and spiritual activities, and would not stimulate the appetite toward gluttony as would meat. He stressed the importance of a simple and inexpensive diet, which is sufficient to satisfy the needs of the body (*Against Jovinianus* 2.10).

Concerning the effect of flesh foods on one's mind, soul, and health, Jerome commented, "Nothing is so destructive to the mind as a full belly, fermenting like a wine vat and giving forth its gases on all sides" (*Against Jovinianus* 2.12). He also remarked, "The soul greatly exults when you are content with little: you have the world beneath your feet, and can exchange all its power, its feasts, and its lusts . . . for common food." And again, "The same food that recovers health, can preserve it, for no one can imagine vegetables to be the cause of disease" (*Against Jovinianus* 2.11).

Jerome, however, never argued for vegetarianism as a rule. He acknowledged the biblical teaching that all foods are permissible (*Against Jovinianus* 2.5). Like many others in the church, he believed that God made all things for our use (*Against Jovinianus* 2.6) and permitted the eating of flesh for non-ascetics, "Let those feed on flesh who serve the flesh, whose bodies boil with desire, who are tied to husbands, and who set their hearts on having off-spring" (*Epistle* 79.7, "To Salvina"). Jerome affirmed that he was not a follower of Pythagoras, since Pythagoras totally abstained from flesh due to transmigration of souls. It is clear that Jerome argued for vegetarianism as a spiritual choice, "And so I too say to you: If you wish to be perfect, it is good not to drink wine, and eat flesh. If you wish to be perfect, it is better to enrich the mind than to stuff the body" (*Against Jovinianus* 2.6). Jerome believed that meat eating stimulated sexual desires, "The eating of flesh, and drinking of wine, and fullness of stomach, is the seed-plot of lust" (*Against Jovinianus* 2.7).

Jerome had much to say about gluttony. He advocated a simple and moderate diet that avoided any heated, provocative, or indigestible dishes, whether meat or vegetable. Jerome even spoke against loading the stomach with vegetables, saying that vegetables are harmless only when taken sparingly and in moderation (*Epistle* 54.10, "To Furia"). He noted that Adam obeyed his belly rather than God and was therefore cast out of paradise, that Satan used hunger to tempt the Lord in the wilderness, that Paul cried, "Meats for the belly and the belly for meats, but God shall destroy both it and them," and that Paul "speaks of the self-indulgent as those 'whose God is their belly.'" Jerome then commented, "Care must be taken, therefore, that abstinence may bring back to Paradise those whom satiety once drove out" *(Epistle* 22:10, "To Eustochium").

Saint Augustine (354–430)

Augustine of Hippo is considered by many to be the greatest theologian of the early church. His theological reflections regarding animals and diet were partly influenced by his prior association with the vegetarian sect of the Manichaeans. Augustine sought to distance himself from the Manichaeans and to prevent Christians from adopting Manichaean doctrines, which among other things forbade the killing of animals (*On the Morals of the Manichaeans* 17.59). Their vegetarianism was based on the superstitious belief that one could heighten spiritual powers and attain divinity by a meatless diet.

Manichaean dualism taught that divine Light was trapped in the earth when it was attacked by Darkness. The Light is able to escape the soil through plant roots and migrate throughout the plant. It is then released as the plants are ground, cooked, chewed, and digested. When animals eat plants they defile the divine Light, since they procreate by the defiling act of sexual intercourse. The Manichaeans believed that celibate holy men, who devote their lives to prayer and fasting, can acquire divinity from eating a diet consisting only of plant food.

In response, Augustine challenged the Manichaean belief that part of God exists in vegetable matter. He also rejected the Manichaean belief that animal food is inherently evil and therefore defiles the souls of those who eat it. It is in this context that we are to understand Augustine's statements about killing animals for food.

> Your abstaining from the slaughter of animals and from injuring plants is shown by Christ to be mere superstition; for, on the ground that there is no community of rights between us and brutes and trees, He both sent the devils into an herd of swine, and withered by His curse a tree in which He had found no fruit. (*On the Morals of the Manichaeans* 17.54)

Augustine interpreted the command "Thou shalt not kill" as pertaining only to humans, not to trees, since they lack feeling, and not to irrational animals, since they lack reason and were appointed by the Creator for our use and to keep us alive (*The City of God* 1.20). In response to the Manichaean prohibition against killing animals Augustine replied that animal suffering was of no concern to humans. He commented, "We see and hear by their cries that animals die with pain, although man disregards this in a beast, with which as not having a rational soul, we have no community of rights" (*On the Morals of the Manichaeans* 17.59). We should note that Augustine is drawing from Greek philosophy (not Hebrew thought) to respond to the Manichaeans.

When Augustine was converted, he adopted a monastic lifestyle that included vegetarianism and celibacy. At Hippo he gathered a small number of monks with him at his "Monastery in the Garden" and continued the practice while serving as priest and bishop. Peter Brown mentions that Augustine "had established an austere monastic routine, with a strict vegetarian diet, and an absolute prohibition on female visitors." However, on his visits to Carthage he would often feast on roast peacock when visiting with important people and colleagues (*Augustine of Hippo*, Univ. of California Press, 1967, pp. 199, 420).

Although Augustine was not a consistent vegetarian, it does appear that he normally abstained from flesh foods. He gave three reasons for abstaining from meat and wine (1) to check indulgence, (2) to protect one's own weak conscience about meat and drink offered to idols, and (3) to show love in not offending others (*On the Morals of the Manichaeans* 14.35).

As with all church fathers, Augustine condemned gluttony. He remarked that we cannot reprove a person for eating meat for health reasons if done without sensual appetite. A person can only be reproved for excess and gluttony. He ridiculed the Manichaeans who do not reprove the one who "gloats with delight over highly-seasoned vegetables, unable to keep possession of himself" (*On the Morals of the Manichaeans* 16.51).

Who Then Ate a Veggie Diet?

Contrary to some of the literature floating about, the early church fathers were not vegetarians of the strictest sort. It may be true of Anthony and perhaps Jerome, but the most that can be said with certainty for the others is that they ate and advocated a simple diet and that the majority probably abstained from meat most of the time. They never insisted on total abstinence from their following but rather allowed liberty in the choice of food. For them to denounce meat eating as absolutely wrong would have been heresy.

The fathers discussed vegetarianism in light of the problems of their day: gnostic dualism and spirituality. Although many were kindhearted toward animals, their discussions did not focus on the ethical issues of animal abuse and exploitation, simply because these were not problems in their culture. Meat eating was a spiritual issue, not a moral issue.

They encouraged a simple lifestyle to aid spirituality and physical health, to curb fleshly lusts and cultivate virtues. With the decline of spirituality and the influx of worldliness and materialism into the modern church, perhaps we need to listen once again to the voices of the church fathers and to their pleas for moderation. In particular, we need to reclaim their practice of training the virtues so as to enhance selfless love toward others within our community.

RECIPES

Macaroni and "Cheese"

2 cups whole wheat elbow macaroni
6 cups water
1 recipe "Cheese" Sauce (chapter 2)
½ cup diced onion (optional)

Bring water to boil. Add the uncooked macaroni and keep boiling for 12 minutes. Drain and pour into an 8x8-inch baking dish. Stir in the "Cheese" Sauce. If adding onions, sauté in small amount of water, drain, and then stir in before baking. Bake uncovered at 350° for 30 minutes.

Spanish Rice

3 cups cooked brown rice
2 cups canned crushed tomatoes with sauce
1 cup cooked and drained pinto beans
1 chopped onion
½ chopped green pepper
½ tsp. each of basil, garlic powder, paprika, oregano, salt

Sauté onion and pepper in small amount of water, drain when done. Then mix all ingredients together and either (1) pour into a large pot and heat on low for about 15 minutes or (2) pour into a baking dish and heat uncovered at 350° for 20 minutes.

12

Will There Be Slaughterhouses in Heaven?

The wolf shall live with the lamb, the leopard shall lie down with the kid, the calf and the lion and the fatling together, and a little child shall lead them. The cow and the bear shall graze, their young shall lie down together; and the lion shall eat straw like the ox. The nursing child shall play over the hole of the asp, and the weaned child shall put its hand on the adder's den. They will not hurt or destroy on all my holy mountain; for the earth will be full of the knowledge of the Lord as the waters cover the sea. (Isaiah 11:6–9)

O God, enlarge within us the sense of fellowship with all living things, our brothers the animals to whom thou gavest the earth as their home in common with us. We remember with shame that in the past we have exercised the high dominion of man with ruthless cruelty so that the voice of the earth, which should have gone up to thee in song, has been a groan of travail. May we realize that they live not for us alone but for themselves and for thee, and that they love the sweetness of life. (St. Basil the Great, cited in *The Complete Book of Christian Prayer,* Continuum, 1996, p. 145)

On our dining room wall we have prints of two of Edward Hicks' paintings, "Noah's Ark" and "The Peaceable Kingdom." The latter depicts Isaiah 11:6–9 with a wolf lying down with a lamb, a leopard lying down with a kid, a little child leading a calf and lion whelp, small children playing with an asp, and a cow and bear grazing together. Hicks relates the biblical story to his own era by including a scene of William Penn making a peace treaty with the Indians. Edward Hicks was an itinerant Quaker preacher and self-taught folk artist who earned a living doing decorative painting on carriages, signs, and furniture during the first half of the nineteenth century. He became obsessed with "The Peaceable Kingdom" and painted over sixty versions of it. For Hicks, it was part of his search for peace within.

After saying grace, we invariably glance once again at the painting hanging on our wall. It is a constant reminder of the direction of our journey and of the Christian hope. It is also a reminder of the story into which we have placed our story. My wife and I do not live by a bunch of absolute rules; nor do we demand that our "rights" be honored. What shapes our lives is a story, and that story is largely depicted by Edward Hicks' painting "The Peaceable Kingdom."

What Is Isaiah Really Saying?

To understand Isaiah's vision of the peaceable kingdom, we need to look at its literary context. Isaiah had encouraged the Israelites not to be afraid of the impending Assyrian invasion. The reason is twofold. First, the Lord God is figuratively portrayed as coming to the aid of Israel and defeating Assyria (Isa 10:24–34). Second, a ruler will appear from the stump of Jesse (indicating the Davidic dynasty) who will lead Israel in righteousness and wisdom (Isa 11:1–5). The wicked will be condemned, and the poor and oppressed will receive justice.

Wherever justice is exercised in perfect righteousness, perfect peace will follow. Isaiah depicts this peace with images reminiscent of Edenic paradise with the leopard and kid lying down together (Isa 11:6–9). The keynote of the passage is the last phrase, "They will not hurt or destroy on all my holy mountain; for the earth will be full of the knowledge of the Lord." This suggests that these conditions flow from knowing God and God's intent for the world, and that failure to understand precipitates disharmony and chaos.

But how literal are we to understand Isaiah's vision? Is the wolf really going to dwell with the lamb? Are the leopard and goat really going to lie down together? Will the lion really eat straw like the ox? It sounds incredible. Perhaps the vision merely symbolizes peaceful coexistence among humans or the renewal of human society. Some suggest it refers to the peaceful reign under Hezekiah, and others to a much future time of human peace. The Israelites, however, always saw the land, animals, and people as an integral unit. What happens to one, happens to the other (cf. Eccl 3:19–21). Isaiah's reflection echoes this motif of solidarity and holistic redemption. If the promises of God were to be meaningful to the Israelites, they had to pertain to all that God loves and cares for. As Claus Westermann says, "A God who is understood only as the god of humankind is no longer the God of the Bible" (p. 176).

Granted, the particulars do sound farfetched. How is it possible for wild carnivorous animals to be otherwise? We have no analogy to evaluate such things. But then the future is a transcendence that lies beyond rational judgment and critique. From a Christian perspective, the future must remain open. To judge the future by analogy to the present would reduce Christian hope to human potential. Christian hope is not the continuation and improvement of the present, but something entirely new—a *novum,* as Jürgen Moltmann calls it.

We must also keep in mind that the prophetic visions are images and part of the symbolic world that gives meaning to our lives. This suggests that we can neither eliminate nor objectify them. Hans Küng remarks that our thoughts about the consummation "must move on the *borderline between image and concept*" (p. 220). Are we then to expect wolves and lambs literally to dwell together and lions actually to eat straw? We simply don't know. What we do know and hope for through the risen Christ is that God will somehow cleanse humans of evil tendencies so that an aura of peace will spread throughout creation.

Living the Resurrection Hope

The Christian faith is to a large extent shaped by the hope of a radically new world. It finds its vitality through envisioning paradise restored, with no more suffering, oppression, sin, and death. Only in this context does Christian faith and life find true meaning and direction. Faith in the resurrection of Christ opens up the future to seemingly incredible possibilities that lie beyond the normal expectations of history. The resurrection of Christ, as Moltmann says, is the "eschatologically new." It does not indicate a new possibility "within the world," but a new possibility "for the world" (p. 179).

Nor was hope for Isaiah mere fantasy. It too was an earnest expectation based on the revelatory acts of God in history. For the Israelites, the exodus was the primary revelatory event that opened up the future for them. The God who led the Israelites out of oppression and bondage in Egypt is the Creator God who is concerned with leading all creatures out of oppression, injustice, and bondage.

The eschatologically new made possible by the resurrection includes the absence of death (Rev 21:4). Moltmann applies this to all God's creatures saying "the fundamental conditions of present creation will be changed." He adds that "modern cynicism which can tolerate the death of so many creatures is a covenant with death. But we Christians are what Christoph Blumhardt called 'protest people against death'" (*History and the Triune God*, Crossroad, 1992, pp. 78, 79).

If on the basis of resurrection hope we anticipate the end of death for God's creatures, then we also anticipate the end of slaughterhouses, the end of intensive animal farms, the end of the fur industry, the end of animal experimentation, and the arrival of universal vegetarianism. Living the resurrection hope is what the Christian life is all about, for as followers of the risen Christ we look to the resurrection as that which gives direction, meaning, hope, and identity to our otherwise bleak existence.

Did Jesus Preach
the Peaceable Kingdom?

The peaceable kingdom should not be divorced from the kingdom of God that was central to the teaching of Jesus, since Hebrew prophecies form the background for much of what Jesus taught. Jesus' teaching, however, represents a radical reinterpretation as well as fulfillment of the kingdom. What Jesus did was to shift the focus of the kingdom from something totally future to something now at hand and accessible, something into which one could enter (Matt 4:17, 23:13). Very few have recognized how radical Jesus' message really is. Jesus is inviting people into the front door of the peaceable kingdom. There are not two kingdoms, only one, and it is the one Jesus preached. There may be different phases of the kingdom, but they are so entwined that one is present in the others.

The kingdom of God speaks of God's rule or kingly authority. As we submit to Christ, we become subjects of the kingdom. The eschatological kingdom then has come upon us and calls for a response. The response is to live as children of the kingdom in anticipation of its future consummation. Practicing the ethics of the kingdom brings a partial realization of the coming of the future into the present. For example, as we treat all God's creatures with love and justice, we can to a limited extent experience what George Ladd calls "the presence of the future."

The story that ends with the peaceable kingdom is none other than the story which Jesus has invited us to enter and participate. It is the kingdom that Jesus taught his disciples to pray for by saying, "Your kingdom come. Your will be done, on earth as it is in heaven" (Matt 6:10). For many it indeed is a strange world, but it is a world that is coming toward us.

Reflections on the Peaceable Kingdom

The peaceable kingdom reflects the Hebrew concept that the history of humanity is inextricably bound with the history of the earth. According to biblical imagery, the present, past, and future of both human and nonhuman creations are on a parallel tract.

Expressed another way, the Scriptures depict a solidarity of all creation. As one part goes, all go. This, of course, runs contrary to human arrogance which exalts humanity above the rest of creation and treats it as a mere resource. In so doing, humans are fracturing the solidarity of creation and undermining their own well-being as well as the well-being of the whole. As Paul Tillich says, "The interdependence of everything with everything else in the totality of being includes a participation of nature in history and demands a participation of the universe in salvation" (*Systematic Theology*, vol. 2, Univ. of Chicago Press, 1967, p. 96).

The Bible clearly depicts the solidarity of creation. Just as animals are implicated in human judgment (Jer 7:20), so will they participate in human restoration (Ps 36:6; Joel 2:21–22). Both humans and animals mourn before God (Jonah 3:6–9) and look to God for sustenance (Ps 104:27–31) and deliverance (Rom 8:18–23). Because of the envisioned solidarity of creation in the peaceable kingdom, vegetarianism may be thought of as the quintessence of the kingdom, as it brings together humans and animals into a community of peace and harmony—the kingdom diet, if you wish.

The peaceable kingdom also envisions an everlasting and all-inclusive peace. Using the image of breaking bows and shattering spears, the psalmist says that the Lord Almighty will eliminate all wars from the face of the earth (Ps 46:9). Isaiah says, "They will beat their swords into plowshares and their spears into pruning hooks. Nation will not take up sword against nation, nor will they train for war anymore" (Isa 2:4 NIV).

The peace, however, is not merely among people. Ezekiel tells us that God will make a covenant of peace that will include both humans and animals. Animals will not kill people, and people will eat from the land rather than eat animals (Ezek 34:25–29). The peace "is a genuine eschatological peace that renews the peace of the beginning, where humans and animals do not depend on one another's destruction for their own survival" (Hauerwas, p. 87). The covenant in Hosea promises that animals will live without fear of being killed and that God will break the bow and sword humans use to kill animals.

> In that day I will make a covenant for them
>> with the beasts of the field and the birds of the air
>> and the creatures that move along the ground.
> Bow and sword and battle
>> I will abolish from the land,
>> so that all may lie down in safety. (Hos 2:18 NIV)

This means that the war against animals will cease. Humans will lay down their weapons—their veal stalls, battery cages, sow gestation crates, slaughterhouses—and there will be war no more.

A third aspect of the peaceable kingdom, as incredible as it may seem, is the cessation of death. Isaiah proclaims that the Lord God "will swallow up death forever" (Isa 25:7). Hosea records God as saying, "I will ransom them from the power of the grave; I will redeem them from death. Where, O death, are your plagues? Where, O grave, is your destruction?" (Hos 13:14 NIV). The resurrection of Christ gave the apostles assurance of future victory over the forces of decay and death (1 Cor 15:26, 54–57). John says that God will wipe away every tear, and there will be no more death (Rev 21:4). If there will be no more death, there will be no more killing. The Hebrew prophets believed that killing of any kind would be antithetical to a peaceable kingdom.

A fourth aspect of the kingdom is liberation. The fulfillment of the kingdom will bring liberation to all creation from the bondage that results from human sin; namely, abuse, tyranny, persecution, victimization, oppression, and exploitation (cf. Isa 65:17–25). The redemption of animals and humans is inseparably bound, for humans will continue to exploit animals and other humans until their own bondage to evil is purged from the heart. God's goal then is not simply the redemption of humanity, but liberation of all creation from bondage to human sin.

A fifth aspect of the peaceable kingdom is that it is located on earth. God's intent is to destroy all that is evil, and the physical world is not evil. What will be purged in the re-creation are those elements that have a corrupting influence on God's creation: evil, sin, disease, and death. Once purged, creation will emerge from the ashes of human arrogance with the pristine beauty of Eden.

This purging is sometimes depicted with the symbol of fire (2 Pet 3:10–13). Irenaeus remarks, "Neither is the substance nor the essence of the creation annihilated (for faithful and true is He who has established it), but 'the *fashion* of the world passeth away;' that is, those things among which transgression has occurred" (*Against Heresies* 5.36.1).

This also conflicts with the received tradition of the church which depicts an ethereal, heavenly habitat of redeemed souls around the throne of God. The received tradition actually reflects a gnostic Platonic view of salvation, not a Hebrew or Christian view. Hans Küng asks, "In this whole tradition—more platonizing than Christian—have not the promises been largely forgotten of a *satisfied nature* and a *satisfied humanity*, as announced for Jews and Christians in the book of Isaiah?" (p. 219). It appears that humans will not have a future devoid of a physical environment. If humanity was designed to be part of an ecosystem, an inner sense of wholeness and fulfillment could never be realized without the corresponding renewal of the community and context of which humans are a part.

Traveling with God on the Journey

We have been called to travel with God on a journey. God is leading us toward a future, where humans and animals coexist in peace, where justice, compassion, and love reign, and where oppression and exploitation are things of the past. God does not coerce us against our wishes. Rather the divine Spirit coaxes and woos us to join God on the journey, to locate our story in God's story, and thereby to see, be, and act as kingdom people.

The question of Christian ethics has always been, How should we act in the world? From a narrative point of view, the answer is informed by another question, What is God up to in the world? The Scriptures tell a grand narrative of what God is doing and where God is headed. It only seems reasonable for those who claim the name of Christ to be heading in the same direction as God. As we journey with God, God's Spirit will use the story to shape our lives, character, and dispositions.

As mentioned earlier, God is headed toward the peaceable kingdom. What God is doing in the world to get there is none other than building a community—a community of creation. But community can never be built if its inhabitants display the vices of pride, covetousness, lust, envy, gluttony, anger, and sloth (the seven deadly sins). These vices issue into such acts as exploitation, oppression, fighting, killing, and war. Instead, community is built on virtues. Classical moral philosophy cited the virtues of temperance, justice, courage, and (practical) wisdom. Christians have added faith, hope, and love, with love being preeminent. Vices are negative relational terms that engender disharmony and division, while virtues are positive relational terms that engender harmony and unity. True community, of course, cannot be built on a forced compliance to an external code of laws. This leaves virtue as the basic ingredient to restore community, and community is the heart of salvation and the essence of the kingdom.

We are heading by God's grace toward a civilized civilization and a humanized humanity. We are heading toward a future in which everything will exist in peace and harmony with itself, the rest of creation, and with the Creator. Christian faith finds meaning and vitality only within this context. To live the Christian life means to be taken up into God's story, to become one with it, and to travel with God on the same path toward the same destination.

A Journey of Protest and Hope

As we travel on our journey, we will be traversing through the destructive wake left behind by a fallen race which is drifting aimlessly ahead. The life of a pilgrim will inevitably contradict such a society with its insensitive toleration of needless death. How can one who is filled with a kingdom hope possibly acquiesce to the customs of a fallen race, with its dietary habits built upon the acceptance of animal abuse and death that arises from the vices of gluttony, selfish desire, and callousness? Resurrection hope rises up in protest against injustice and needless carnage wherever it is found. Moltmann remarks,

Those who hope in Christ can no longer put up with reality as it is, but begin to suffer under it, to contradict it. Peace with God means conflict with the world, for the goad of the promised future stabs inexorably into the flesh of every unfulfilled present. (*Theology of Hope*, p. 21)

In light of the resurrection hope, it is impossible to tolerate animal abuse, exploitation, and oppression. The risen Christ, as Moltmann says, is the enemy "of a world that puts up with death" (*Theology of Hope*, p. 21). Hope must issue forth in protest against a world that is out of sync with God's promises and that condones needless killing of animals for self-gratification.

However, we must be cautious about turning the eschatological hope into an absolute rule. The end of the story gives meaning and direction to the rest of the story and as such becomes a dominant element in shaping our character and the way we view the world. We see the world eschatologically, from the end of the story. But the end is still part of the narrative, and the narrative functions as a guideline for the journey. The end cannot be applied universally as an absolute moral precept. Departures from God's path become morally wrong and occasions for Christian protest only within specific circumstances as vices emerge from within.

We may be living in a fallen world, but we are also living in the shadow of the resurrection. The resurrection is both a victory over and a protest against suffering, injustice, and death. The resurrection has opened up the future to possibilities that defy the imagination. In viewing history in the light of the resurrection, we should no longer speak of ideals, but rather of promise and hope. The resurrection has actualized the ideals and turned them into promises. No longer do we think as the Greeks, with unattainable ideals, but as the Israelites who were always on the *move* toward the promise. This means that we can no longer put up with the world as it is, with its acceptance of animal abuse and killing. No longer can we be content with God's concession to eat meat. If the resurrection of Christ has any meaning for the Christian, it means that a new creation has begun and that our lives are to be lived as much as humanly possible in a radically new way through the power of the Holy Spirit.

The End of Slaughterhouses

In summary, the peaceable kingdom is neither an extension of human kingdoms nor the product of human utopianism. It is a *novum* brought about by divine initiative. It speaks of the cessation of all wars, bloodshed, sin, violence, oppression, exploitation, and hatred upon the earth. It speaks of totality, wholeness, completion, harmony, security, well-being, friendship, and community. The peaceable kingdom encompasses the full range of human moral aspirations, depicts peaceful coexistence between humans and nonhumans, and represents the goal toward which God is guiding history.

Although we would like to see kingdom living practiced throughout creation, we must recognize that others cannot see the world through the lens of the resurrection without personal transformation. Rather than directly imposing her agenda on the world, the church should be content with being a living community of faith, manifesting the kingdom in word and deed to a watching world. It means that the church is to be the church by living God's story as much as possible. Faithfully living the story in the midst of a contrary society is a form of protest which indirectly can invoke change. Just think of what would happen if all Christians suddenly became vegetarian.

The church then is not to become a front organization for vegetarianism or animal rights. The reason the church must maintain her traditional focus on individual repentance and faith is that the problem of animal abuse is part of the larger problem of human cruelty in general that issues from the vices of selfishness, greed, and the like. The church clearly has a role to play as we move into the future. Our task is to be faithful to God's story of salvation and promise, guide people toward inner transformation, and to leave the final outcome in God's hands. As we follow God's path, we will help make the present world a better place to live for all God's creatures.

R E C I P E S

Heavenly Stew

    1 large onion, quartered and cut into 1-inch slices
    3 carrots, cut into ½-inch chunks
    3 medium potatoes, peeled and cut into ¾-inch chunks
    2 celery stalks, cut into ¾-inch chunks
    2 medium zucchini, cut into ¾-inch chunks
    2 cups water
    1 8-oz. can tomato sauce (or 1 cup chunky tomato sauce)
    1 Tbs. soy sauce
    1 Tbs. parsley flakes
    1 tsp. salt
    ½ tsp. each basil, paprika, garlic powder
    1 bay leaf

Cook first five ingredients in 2 cups water until almost tender. Then add rest of ingredients and simmer for 20 to 30 minutes more.

Granola Cookies/Bars

    1 cup whole pitted dates
    1 cup orange (or other) juice
    1½ cups rolled oats
    ½ cup each whole wheat flour, soy flour (or white flour),
        shredded coconut, chopped walnuts, raw sunflower
        seeds, and raisins
    1 Tbs. blackstrap molasses
    2 tsp. coriander
    ½ tsp. salt

Cut dates into pieces and whiz in blender with orange juice until creamy. Mix the remaining ingredients in a large bowl and then stir in the date mixture, adding more water as needed to be able to form cookies. Moisten hands with water and pat out mixture on a cutting board to about ⅜-inch thickness and cut with glass or cookie cutter into 2½-inch wide cookies. Lift with metal spatula unto oiled cookie sheet and bake at 350° for 25 minutes. Could also be made into Granola Bars.

13

What Then Shall We Eat?

Some judge one day to be better than another, while others judge all days to be alike. Let all be fully convinced in their own minds. Those who observe the day, observe it in honor of the Lord. Also those who eat, eat in honor of the Lord, since they give thanks to God; while those who abstain, abstain in honor of the Lord and give thanks to God. (Romans 14:5–8)

I was early convinced in my mind that true religion consisted in an inward life, wherein the heart doth love and reverence God the Creator, and learns to exercise true justice and goodness, not only toward all men, but also toward the brute creatures; that, as the mind was moved by an inward principle to love God as an invisible, incomprehensible Being, so, by the same principle, it was moved to love Him in all his manifestations in the visible world; that, as by his breath the flame of life was kindled in all animal sensible creatures, to say we love God as unseen, and at the same time exercise cruelty toward the least creature moving by his life, or by life derived from Him, was a contradiction in itself. (*The Journal of John Woolman*, Harvard Classics, 1937, p. 173)

While we have been called to travel with God on the journey, what we eat is a matter of individual spiritual choice; it is not something legislated by divine decree. God is not a legalistic despot who demands conformity to a set of rules. What we have in the Bible are not absolute laws that demand perfect conformity, but a story that gives general orientation. Throughout the biblical narrative are directional markers that point toward the peaceable kingdom. By functioning as general guidelines for the journey, these pointers do allow space for us to roam about. This means that eating meat is not wrong in and of itself even though it is contrary to the direction of the story. God's grace allows us freedom to trek our own haphazard way through the Christian life. Along with the freedom, however, comes the responsibility to be faithful to the story and to allow the story to shape our lives.

Directional Markers for the Journey

The path is well marked with signposts. The story not only tells us about the points of origin and destination but also provides pointers along the way. These pointers include such images as the cross, resurrection, community, renewal and restoration, healing, peace and harmony, and the imitation of God. They function both as symbols of our faith to give meaning to our lives and as directional markers to provide orientation for our journey. The pointers all converge at the destination.

First, the cross signifies divine forgiveness, God's self-giving love for the world, and God's joining the ranks of the suffering and oppressed throughout creation. The story of the suffering God gives consolation and hope to all who suffer, both humans and animals, for it says that God is with them and for them. One unmistakable theme of the Hebrew prophets is that God sides with the oppressed. The cross points us in the direction of self-giving love that takes sides with the suffering, victimized, exploited, and oppressed, whether human or animal.

Second, the resurrection of Christ is a message of hope to all who suffer. The resurrection opens up the future to new possibilities and revitalizes the visions of Eden. The impossible is now possible. The resurrection is the initial act in the new creation and the turning point in God's narrative. Christ's victory over the forces of exploitation and oppression promises universal peace, righteousness, and justice throughout creation. The message of the risen Christ instills in us a living hope that transforms the way we think and act toward all God's creatures.

Third, community is what the kingdom is all about. Christians normally limit community to "church," a community of disciples following Christ. However, our present context calls for a restructuring of the symbol so that we can speak of a community within a community. Community in its broadest sense refers to mending and maintaining relationships throughout creation. The biblical story tells us that God created and is restoring a *creation community*. This may be a hard pill for many Christians to swallow, but it suggests that, in the spirit of Saint Francis, the sow shut up in the gestation crate is our sister, the calf confined in a veal cage is our brother, and the mice and rabbits in the laboratories are our cousins. And yes, even those who operate the fur farms, animal factories, and laboratories are our brothers and sisters.

Fourth, the notion of renewal is embedded deep within Hebrew thought. The Israelites were a suffering and oppressed people on the move toward the hopes and promises that lay before them. They looked for the renewal of individuals, their nation, the world, and all creation. Peter spoke of the restoration of *all things* that was promised long before through the prophets (Acts 3:21). The cosmic scope of Messianic renewal is commonly recognized by Jewish scholars. Abraham Isaac Kook says, "Every defect is destined to be mended. Thus we are assured that the day will come when creation will return to its original state" (*The Lights of Penitence*, Paulist, 1978, p. 59). For Kook this means a return to vegetarianism. From a Christian perspective, we are now living in the times of the Messiah, and the process of renewal has begun.

The process of renewal, in which promises become actualized, has begun with Christ's victory over sin and death. Paul says, "If anyone is in Christ, he is a new creation; the old has gone, the new has come" (2 Cor 5:17 NIV). This suggests that the context that provoked the concession to eat meat in Genesis 9 is beginning to change. The divine concession to eat meat was given during an age of rampant violence throughout the earth. Violence certainly continues, but Christians are called to participate in a resurrection faith that arises above violence. By participating we begin to see, think, and act differently. Like the Israelites, Christians are people of hope on a journey toward the promised future. The concession is a thing of the past.

Fifth, healing in the biblical context as well as in contemporary thought is holistic. Jesus, for example, healed both physical ailments and infirmities of the soul. The Hebrew prophets commonly linked the spiritual and moral depravity of the people with the languishing of the land and animals (cf. Hosea 4:1–3). This suggests that we are relational beings existing in a rather extensive community; when one member suffers, the whole suffers (cf. 1 Cor 12:26). In modern parlance we speak of the interconnectedness of all life, suggesting that one cannot really be healthy when the environment is sick. If there is to be healing, it must be relational and involve the whole. This is clearly the direction of the biblical narrative. The biblical story points us in the direction of healing relations and restoring community throughout creation.

Sixth, the images of peace and harmony not only bracket the biblical narrative on both ends in Genesis and Revelation but also are dispersed throughout the story. The Hebrew prophets often speak about swords being turned into plowshares and spears into pruning hooks. This peace is for humans and animals alike. Isaiah speaks of peace in the animal kingdom (11:6–9, 65:25). Hosea speaks of a covenant that abolishes weapons used against animals (2:18). Job also speaks of animals being at peace with humans (5:23). Paul speaks about animals being liberated from bondage (Rom 8:21).

To limit peace to an inner spiritual tranquility before God, as is often done in Christian circles, reflects a gnostic dualism that ignores the integrity of creation. Embracing vegetarianism as a spiritual choice makes a compelling statement that Christians are ambassadors of peace in a broken world, take seriously their belief in the resurrection, and live in light of God's promise of cosmic reconciliation and renewal.

Finally, the imitation of God *(imitatio Dei)* or Christ *(imitatio Christi)* has long been a model and goal of Christian piety and spirituality. Imaging God, however, is more of a way of life than a rule of life, for it is rather difficult to command a change in character. Even though we are exhorted, "Be holy, for I am holy" (Lev 11:44), we cannot reduce the image of God to abstract principles or rules that exist apart from the narrative. We observe divine virtues by witnessing divine activity in the story. As we enter the story through repentance and faith and participate through the Holy Spirit, we begin to reflect God's virtues and image (2 Pet 1:4).

God's character does not consist of those traits that engender murder. God exists as a social being, a trinity of persons in perfect unity. The disposition that makes this impossible notion possible reflects the virtues of love and justice. The vices that engender murder (such as pride, covetousness, lust, envy, and anger) simply cannot be part of a perfect social being. While killing our fellow creatures may be necessary at times in our dysfunctional world, the divine image points us away from all such killing. One cannot fully image God and continue to kill for food when not necessary, for killing is contrary to the very being of God as well as to the divine narrative.

Our character is shaped as we walk with the Spirit in the direction of the story. The directional markers in the story point the way and guide in the formation of virtues. As virtues are formed, our conduct will invariably change.

Formation of Virtues

The story helps shape our inner attitudes, character, and virtues. We appropriate the virtues of love and compassion as we follow in the spirit of God's love for the world and Jesus' love in giving his life for others. We appropriate the virtue of hope as we follow in the spirit of the prophets who anticipated a renewal of creation and in the spirit of Jesus whose resurrection promises a new beginning. We appropriate the virtue of justice when we follow in the spirit of God's siding with the oppressed. Virtues are formed within as we place our story in God's story and begin traveling with God on the journey in the power of the Holy Spirit.

"Traveling on the journey" and "participating in the story" are contemporary metaphors for the ancient idea of training the virtues. The author of Hebrews comments that the mature are those "whose faculties have been trained by practice to distinguish good from evil" (Heb 5:14). But training is not simply a matter of living a story. Biblical writers consistently testify that it is God who transforms the inner life. For example, David writes, "Create in me a clean heart, O God, and put a new and right spirit within me" (Ps 51:10). The formation of virtue then involves discipline, direction, and cooperation with God. Roberta Bondi tells how Origen of Alexandria explains the relationship:

> It is like traveling in a sailing ship on the ocean. Our life is like the ship, and we are the captain. All our skill, energy, and attention are necessary to avoid shipwreck and arrive at the port, for the ocean is dangerous and inattention is disastrous upon it. Our ship, however, also needs the wind. It is the wind that fills the sails and moves the ship, and when the two are weighed against each other, the skill of the captain seems very small compared with the contribution of the wind. (p. 35)

Generally speaking, *who* we are determines *how* we act. That is, being precedes act. Thus the essence of the Christian moral life is an inner transformation of the person into a new creature—right conduct generally follows. Rules are not really in the picture except as guidelines.

Many will respond, "But isn't the essence of the Christian moral life obedience?" "Isn't the Bible full of laws, rules, and commands to obey?" Yes, much of it is. Laws under the old covenant were external. They were laid upon us from without. As we analyze the specific situations in which the laws were formulated, we will find that they are simply contextualized ways of encouraging people to follow God. Most laws given under the old covenant still function for us as general pointers along the way.

With the coming of the Messiah, Christians affirm that the New Covenant has been inaugurated (Heb 8:8–13). God's laws are no longer etched on tables of stone, but inscribed on the heart. They go beyond rules and principles to the formation of Christian character that reflects the very nature and being of God. The metaphor of God's laws being inscribed on the heart is a figurative way of saying that the Holy Spirit purges vices and molds virtues in the human heart.

In the Sermon on the Mount, Jesus shifted the focus to inner dispositions that will naturally fulfill the demands of the law. This shift is quite significant for understanding the Christian moral life. How is it possible for our righteousness to exceed that of the scribes and Pharisees, except by locating morality in the heart rather than in external observances (Matt 5:20)? After encouraging us to greater righteousness, Jesus begins his famous series of reversals in which morality is lodged primarily in one's dispositions.

The shift in focus back to a rule-based Christianity may partially be due to the influence of modern thinking with its desire to objectify faith and practice. Many Christians assimilated modern rationality into their theology when responding to the Enlightenment challenge and accordingly reduced the faith to rational propositions and practice to objective rules. Virtues took a back seat as rules took over driving Christian morality.

Virtue ethics is rather old, going back to Aristotle and Plato. Both reject the notion of universally valid rules or principles and teach that moral or immoral conduct issues from inner states (virtues and vices). But moral or noble actions for Aristotle are partially based on the situation, whereas for Plato they are based entirely on one's attitude. This is an important distinction for our following discussions. Aquinas developed classical virtue ethics from a Christian perspective, teaching that virtues are formed by habit and that one can discern what to do in any given situation through practical judgment guided by inner virtues. There has been much recent thought about virtue ethics that seeks to develop the themes of Aristotle, Plato, and Aquinas for our present day.

Decision Making

In the Introduction we said that the difference between most other ethical theories and virtue ethics can be summarized respectively by the questions, What am I to do? and What am I to be? However, the matter is not quite that simple. We do not simply "be," but we "be" in community. This means learning about our community and listening to its diverse voices in order to determine what constitutes virtuous conduct in our highly complicated society.

Virtues are always formed and expressed within a community. In the biblical text quoted at the beginning of this chapter, Paul encourages his readers to decide for themselves whether they are to eat meat or abstain. But that decision was to be done before God and with regard to the community in which they belonged. Later in that chapter he says, "It is good not to eat meat or drink wine or do anything that makes your brother or sister stumble" (Rom 14:21).

While virtues lie at the base of Christian morality, the world is too complex to simply let the virtues flow. Yes, the virtues are trained through practice and habit. And yes, trained virtues will naturally express themselves in noble conduct in simple situations. But here we run into a snag. We live in an incredibly complex society. We live in dynamic interaction with the rest of creation, affecting it and being affected by it. What we do sends ripples throughout creation. Our overindulging in meat, for example, contributes to the overall impact of intensive animal factories on soil erosion and water pollution, and even contributes to rain forest destruction and the worsening of socioeconomic conditions of indigenous peoples in Third World countries. These in turn send ripples in other directions, so that eventually we all suffer—plants, animals, and humans alike.

Our complex world demands a decision-making process. Since virtues are expressed in community, we must listen to various voices within our community, including those of our nonhuman parishioners. How do we, as pilgrims on the journey, express the virtues of love, compassion, hope, and justice in our present community, with its animal factories and laboratories? Making moral decisions involves listening to the biblical narrative, paying attention to contemporary voices, following one's virtues, being sensitive to the Holy Spirit, and maintaining a good conscience before God.

Can Eating Meat Ever Become Wrong?

One would expect that without an external set of absolute rules, one would not be able to judge whether an act is right or wrong. This is hardly the case. We observed in chapter 6 that the prophetic denouncements against meaningless sacrifices were based on virtue ethics. In the context of ancient Israel, animal sacrifice was an acceptable mode of worship. What made sacrifice wrong was a disobedient and unfaithful attitude on the part of the worshipers. When sacrifice was reduced to empty formalism, it became tantamount to murder and something that the Hebrew prophets vigorously condemned as wrong.

The same can be applied to the eating of meat. While killing animals for food is contrary to the direction of the story, it is not wrong in and of itself. What potentially makes meat eating wrong is gluttony, lust, callousness, arrogance, and the like. Virtues express themselves in right and noble conduct, while vices express themselves in wrong and base conduct. Christians have every right to protest against cruel, insensitive, and barbaric slaughter of animals, for it grotesquely reflects the vices of a fallen race that has lost its way. It reflects a disrespect for God and a lack of love and compassion for God's creation.

Do we then go around condemning anyone who eats meat? No. Consumers do not purchase their neatly wrapped cellophane packages of meat at the grocery with a cold, calloused heart against animals. Nor do they sit down to a meal of steak or chicken with a murderous attitude. Most people are very affectionate toward animals and grieve over their death. However, relatively few are aware of the cruelty and suffering that factory-farmed animals have to endure. If consumers personally had to raise animals with the torturous methods of intensive animal farming and then personally slaughter the animals they ate, very few would continue to eat meat. They would recognize that abusive treatment of animals is morally wrong and would have no part in it. Yet unwittingly they are abetting one of the most hideous industries humanity has ever devised.

We can, however, call people to task for indulging in gluttony. Today's inordinate consumption of meat would probably be viewed as gluttony by the biblical writers and early church fathers. Overindulging in meat because it delights the senses or gives airs of social acceptability emanates from inner vices and can be condemned as wrong. But what about moderate or sparse consumption? Perhaps it is not wrong in and of itself, but collectively it all adds up to a rather huge demand on the market.

The enormous demand for meat has necessitated intensive animal factories to fulfill the need. There is simply no other way to do it. Animal factories are unquestionably cruel operations that completely ignore the sanctity of animal life. But if vices lie at the base of wrong action, where are the vices located? We cannot say that the corporate owners or plant managers are solely responsible. That would be grossly unfair. Yes, some may be driven by greed, and others may have become a bit calloused by their involvement, but that is only part of the picture. It is consumers who drive the production. This means that both the consumer and producer are members of one vast institution. What we are talking about then is institutional violence and institutional vice. While people may not eat factory-farmed meat with a calloused heart, partaking unwittingly implicates them in an institution that does have a calloused heart.

The situation even becomes more serious if the consumer is fully aware of the atrocities taking place in the animal factories. Would picking up that nicely wrapped cellophane package any longer be merely an innocent act? Is the cellophane package simply another product or has it now become the remains of a fellow resident who wanted to live and enjoy life? Would partaking continue the needless suffering of God's creatures?

How is one to live virtuously in such a situation? Paul offers a solution to this quandary with his discussion in Romans 14 about exercising Christian liberty. One has freedom to eat meat or abstain (that is, there are no rules that govern Paul's situation), but the decision must be made with regard to one's community, the direction of one's story, and in accordance with one's conscience before God.

Closing Reflections

The Bible neither commands nor condemns vegetarianism. It is left as a choice. However, as we locate our story in God's story, it is difficult to avoid the implication that vegetarianism is the best dietary choice for Christians. As Alasdair MacIntyre says, "I can only answer the question 'What am I to do?' if I can answer the prior question 'Of what story or stories do I find myself a part'" (p. 201).

But as mentioned earlier, the Bible contains many stories— some heading toward the kingdom and others heading off in different directions. The question we must close with is, What story is shaping our identity? Is it the story about a concession to the fallen human condition or is it the story about a new life made possible by the risen Christ? We have found that vegetarianism is an orientation to the world that corresponds to the very essence and direction of the overarching biblical story, an orientation that speaks of selfless love, peace, community, wholeness, justice, and healing. This leads Francis X. Clooney to remark, "The choice to become a vegetarian can be a prudent and religious one, founded in values not alien to our tradition" ("Vegetarianism and Religion," *America*, Feb. 1979, p. 134).

If meat eating is part of a fallen world, then we must seriously consider vegetarianism to be the dietary choice of one who has entered the kingdom and seeks to travel with God on the journey into the promised future. How can one who places hope in the possibilities opened up by the risen Christ continue a predatory lifestyle? A meatless diet can bring substantial healing to our devastated environment, mend shattered relations within the creation community, and help restore our deteriorated physical and spiritual condition. The choice is between a meat-eating diet that celebrates a fallen world or a vegetarian diet that celebrates new life through the risen Christ.

Moreover, recent research into vegetarian nutrition has indirectly reduced the standard meat-based diet to an unnecessary luxury. If meat-eating is unnecessary, then why subject animals to unnecessary suffering, the environment to unnecessary degradation, and our own bodies to unnecessary health risks just to satisfy our lust for succulent foods? Could it be that our egocentric habits are driving the wedge of separation deeper into an already fragmented world thereby obscuring even more the meaning that comes through love and community?

The vegetarian meal is a celebration of life in which we permit our fellow creatures to experience the joy of existence that God graciously shared with us and our companions. It beckons us to a gentler, kinder way of life that exemplifies the Christian hope. My prayer is that our daily meals will become spiritual activities that celebrate the wonders and mysteries of God and God's creation.

R E C I P E S

Fudgy Brownies

> 1 cup oat flour (dry blend rolled oats)
> ¾ cup whole pitted dates
> ¾ cup apple juice (or water)
> 1 cup whole wheat flour
> ¾ cup chopped walnuts
> ½ cup carob powder
> ½ tsp. salt
> ¾ cup vanilla flavored soy milk (or water)

Dry blend rolled oats to make oat flour. Cut up dates to be sure all pits are removed and then blend in ¾ cup apple juice until creamy. Mix all dry ingredients together in bowl and then add date mixture and ¾ cup soy milk, mixing thoroughly. Spread into an oiled 8x8-inch dish and bake at 350° for 30 minutes. When done, top with frosting (below), let stand awhile, then cut into squares.

Carob-Coconut Frosting

¾ cup vanilla flavored soy milk
2 Tbs. carob powder
2 Tbs. cornstarch
¼ cup turbinado sugar (or brown sugar)
½ cup coconut

Heat first four ingredients in saucepan until thickened, stirring constantly with wire whisk. Then stir in coconut. Spread over the brownies.

Epilogue

Going
Vegetarian

As mentioned in the Preface, our personal journey into vegetarianism was quite gradual. One of the reasons was that we were not sure if it would be nutritionally complete. At first we questioned whether we would be getting enough protein and energy from our diet. After reading several books and articles on the topic, our anxiety was eased. Milk was a bit harder. Would we really be getting enough calcium? Laura was especially concerned, as she was approaching the age when calcium was a particular concern for women. Even after listening to John McDougall's presentation and reading his books, we were still a bit apprehensive. We continued to investigate the matter.

The thought that kept plaguing us was that if the people in China can live a healthy life on very little meat and no milk, then why couldn't we? An epidemiological study of 6,500 people in rural China conducted by Dr. T. Colin Campbell of Cornell University demonstrated that the Chinese diet is much healthier than the typical American diet, with much less heart disease, cancer, and virtually no cases of osteoporosis.

We also realized that our attitudes toward diet had been conditioned by our culture. We live in a highly competitive economic society with large numbers of special interest groups protecting their stakes through lobbying, mass media campaigns, and financial contributions to politicians and research. One reason people in the United States question the adequacy of a vegetarian diet is because they have accepted the propaganda of the meat and dairy industries.

Large numbers of vegetarians have lived long, healthy lives; some of whom have lived to be 100 years and older. Those who adopt a vegetarian diet testify that they feel healthier and younger than when they ate meat. Modern nutritional research is bearing out this personal testimony with evidence that a vegetarian diet is not only adequate but even healthier than a meat-based diet.

Another hesitation about going vegetarian was not knowing how to plan a healthy diet. We discovered that a nutritious vegetarian diet is not the standard American diet minus meat. A vegetarian diet cannot be haphazard. As with all healthy diets, it calls for basic nutritional knowledge and proper planning. The American Dietetic Association has concluded that vegetarian diets are healthful and nutritionally adequate when appropriately planned (*Journal of the American Dietetic Association* 93:11, November 1993).

As we will see, it is really quite simple to plan a healthy vegetarian diet. The key is variety. One needs to eat from a wide variety of plant foods, with plenty of vegetables and whole grains, moderate amounts of fruits and legumes, and a small amount of nuts and seeds. It should be a diet high in complex carbohydrates and dietary fiber, modest amounts of protein, and low in fats. Health conscious persons also recommend limiting the intake of sweets, salt, and refined foods and eliminating eggs and dairy products.

The more we restricted our diet, the more we had to be concerned with getting all the nutrients we need. We had particular concerns with getting enough vitamin B_{12}, vitamin D, calcium, iron, and quality protein. These concerns are much greater for vegetarians who avoid all animal products than it is for vegetarians who still eat milk and eggs, for the latter can obtain protein, calcium, and B_{12} from dairy and egg sources.

Vitamin B_{12}

Vitamin B_{12} is found almost exclusively in animal foods (meat, eggs, and milk). Getting enough B_{12} therefore is a special concern for vegetarians who eliminate eggs and dairy products from their diet. B_{12} is not actually produced by animals, but rather by microorganisms, such as bacteria and algae that live in the host organism.

Some plant foods, however, contain B_{12}, such as seaweeds (e.g., kelp), soy products that use microorganisms in their production (e.g., soy sauce, miso, and tempeh), and vegetables that are not completely washed. These are not reliable sources since the amount and kind of B_{12} present depend on how the food is processed. Tempeh, for example, contains mostly inactive B_{12}, called "analogues." The inactive form of B_{12} interferes with the absorption of the active form. T. Colin Campbell claims that plants can absorb B_{12} from microorganisms in the soil, but this is debatable.

The Recommended Daily Allowance of B_{12} is very small, only two micrograms per day. Many authorities believe that one microgram per day is sufficient. Also, the body can store B_{12} for five years or more.

Vitamin B_{12} deficiency is a very serious problem, as it leads to irreversible nerve damage, a reduction in the number of red blood cells, and gastrointestinal disturbances. This condition is known as pernicious anemia. It is primarily caused by the body's inability to absorb the vitamin. Very few recorded cases are due to dietary deficiency. People who eat animal foods, and therefore have surplus B_{12} in their diet, develop pernicious anemia much more frequently than total vegetarians. Less than a dozen diet-related cases of "B_{12} deficiency have been reported among the tens of millions of vegetarians in the world" (McDougall, *Program*, p. 46).

One possible reason for the scarcity of B_{12} deficiency among total vegetarians is that enough usable B_{12} may be produced by bacteria in the mouth and intestines. Another possible reason could be that the body is quite efficient at reabsorbing the B_{12} it secretes from its reserves into the small intestines. Because these reasons are not certain and because deficiency can result in irreversible nerve damage, it is wise for total vegetarians and vegans to supplement B_{12} in their diets from reliable sources.

Supplements are found in fortified foods, such as some soy milks, cereals (Nutri-Grain and Grape-Nuts), and Red Star T-6635+ nutritional yeast flakes (1 to 2 teaspoons daily meets the adult RDA). The B_{12} in the Red Star yeast contains active B_{12}. Nutritional yeast is different from brewers yeast, and its flake form is often used in making non-dairy cheese sauces. However, too much B_{12} could be harmful.

Calcium and Vitamin D

Although the body needs calcium, the need for milk products has been greatly misrepresented by the milk industry and the National Dairy Council. Mass advertisements that state "everybody needs milk" and "eggs do not increase the risk of heart attack" have been called into question as false and misleading propaganda. Consumers generally believe that dairy products are essential to maintain adequate calcium intake and prevent osteoporosis. Even many doctors regularly tell their patients, especially post-menopausal women, to drink milk.

If the total vegetarian diet is properly planned, calcium dietary deficiency is not a problem. McDougall comments, *"Calcium deficiency of dietary origin is unknown in humans"* (*Program*, p. 48). Granted, there is a higher concentration of calcium in milk than other foods, but hardly any food is devoid of calcium. Calcium is one of the most common elements on our planet and is almost ubiquitous in plant foods. Some plant foods have only a trace, while others are quite rich.

Foods high in calcium include dark leafy green vegetables (e.g., collards, kale, and spinach), broccoli, rhubarb, blackstrap molasses, dried figs, sunflower seeds, butternut squash, and many beans (especially pinto, black, great northern, navy, garbanzo, and soybeans). Although not as high a percentage as in dairy milk, calcium from these sources can be sufficient for a vegan and total vegetarian diet. One cup of cooked collards, for example, has about the same amount of calcium as one eight-ounce glass of whole milk. Other good sources of calcium include fortified soy milks, calcium fortified orange juice, and some tofu processed with calcium sulfate (check the labels).

The amount of calcium that is absorbed is regulated by the body. When the intake of calcium is low, the body absorbs a greater percentage from what is consumed. When the intake is high, the body absorbs a lower percentage, excreting the excess. Vitamin D is necessary for calcium absorption. The body synthesizes vitamin D from exposure to the sun and then stores it in the body. Researchers have determined that three twenty-minute exposures to the sun each week from spring to fall is sufficient for a year's supply. Since vitamin D is readily obtained from moderate exposure to the sun, it does not need to be supplied by fortified milk. Office or factory workers with little exposure to sunlight might need vitamin D supplements.

As mentioned in earlier chapters, studies are now showing that osteoporosis is not a disease arising from calcium deficiency in the diet. The amount of calcium taken in from dairy products has little affect on osteoporosis. Instead, what the studies demonstrate is that when animal protein intake is high, more calcium is excreted in the urine than is taken in through the diet. This extra calcium must be taken from the reserves in the body (i.e., bones). Thus the best defense against osteoporosis is not more calcium in the diet, but less animal protein. The problem seems to be with animal protein's high concentration of sulfur-containing amino acids (cf. McDougall, *Plan*, pp. 102–3; *Program*, pp. 48, 382–84; Barnard, pp. 18–21).

It should be noted that cows and oxen get enough calcium from vegetable foods to build very strong bones. This reminds us of the episode Henry David Thoreau once related:

> One farmer says to me, "You cannot live on vegetable food solely, for it furnishes nothing to make bones with;" and so he religiously devotes a part of his day to supplying his system with the raw material of bones; walking all the while he talks behind his oxen, which, with vegetable-made bones, jerk him and his lumbering plow along in

spite of every obstacle. (*The Annotated Walden,* Clarkson N. Potter, 1970, p. 151)

Iron

Most people in Western societies depend on meat for their iron source. When meat is removed from the diet, one may be susceptible to iron-deficiency anemia. Anemia results in a reduction of the hemoglobin in the bloodstream and thus a reduction in the amount of oxygen carried to the tissues and the amount of carbon dioxide carried back to the lungs.

Vegetarians must obtain their iron from plant foods. Plant foods rich in iron include legumes, kale, collards, dried fruit, tofu, whole-wheat flour, sunflower seeds, most nuts (not peanut butter), and blackstrap molasses. However, there is a difference in iron. Forty percent of the iron from animal sources is heme iron, which is absorbed more readily than iron from plant sources (nonheme iron). Vitamin C enhances the absorption of nonheme iron. Cooking in iron cookware also increases iron content in the diet.

Quality Protein

The idea that meat protein gives us strength is an ancient myth that links meat eating with male dominance, aggression, and power. Our energy supply does not primarily come from protein; it comes from carbohydrates (and fats). Protein is converted into energy only when carbohydrates are not available. On a carbohydrate-based diet, one does not have to worry about a lack of energy. There have been many successful athletes, including weight lifters, wrestlers, cyclists, and marathon runners who were strict vegetarians and who derived their energy from complex carbohydrates.

The body does need protein, but not for energy. It uses protein for growth, tissue repair, and hormone and enzyme production. Although humans vary in their protein needs, hardly anyone needs as much as is commonly consumed in affluent countries.

Authorities now say that only ten percent of our daily calorie intake needs to be protein. Excess protein is not stored in the body, but is passed through the kidneys and is excreted as waste. High protein diets cause unnecessary stress on the kidneys, sometimes leading to kidney failure. Excess protein has also been implicated in liver problems and osteoporosis. The dangers of excess protein could even be a problem with vegetarians who consume large amounts of vegetable protein (legumes).

The body makes protein from twenty amino acids. The body can synthesize all but nine of these building blocks of human protein. These nine are called essential amino acids and must be obtained from foods. If one of the nine is absent, protein cannot be formed in the body. Animal protein (meat, dairy, eggs) contains all nine of these essential amino acids in fairly good proportions. Many plant foods also have all nine essential amino acids, but the level of each amino acid varies with each food. In general, legumes are higher in the essential amino acids in which grains are lower, and vice versa.

This observation led to a misconception about getting enough balanced protein in a vegetarian diet. Frances Moore Lappé in *Diet for a Small Planet* (1971) recommended that vegetarians combine various foods at the same meal that complement each other's amino acid deficiencies. Food combining is naturally practiced in many traditional cultures which exist mostly on legumes and grains, such as the bean and tortilla diet of Latin American countries, the falafel or hummus with pita bread in the Middle East, or a soy product with rice as in Asian countries. The ratio of grain to legume in these traditional diets is approximately 75 to 25.

In her tenth anniversary edition Lappé revised her previous comments about protein complementing. She notes that there is no danger of protein deficiency in a varied vegetable diet. Protein deficiency could be a problem in diets that are heavily dependent on single types of food, such as fruit or junk foods. She states, *"In all other diets, if people are getting enough calories, they are virtually certain of getting enough protein"* (*Diet for a Small Planet*, Ballantine, 1982, p. 162). Food combining to achieve an adequate supply of balanced protein is no longer considered necessary. One should make sure that good sources of vegetable protein are included in the daily diet (e.g., whole grains, legumes, seeds, and nuts) and that the diet contains enough calories to maintain energy.

McDougall even says, "All the essential and nonessential amino acids are represented in *single unrefined starches* such as rice, corn, wheat, and potatoes in amounts in excess of every individual's needs, even if they are endurance athletes or weight lifters" (*Program*, p. 45). Victor Herbert, writing in *The Mount Sinai School of Medicine Complete Book of Nutrition*, comments, "Any adult vegetarian who consumes adequate calories from a wide variety of nutritious foods is almost certain to meet protein needs also" (p. 419).

Plants synthesize amino acids from the environment, animals do not. Animals are therefore dependent on plant food either directly or indirectly for protein. Herbivores, such as oxen and horses, obtain plenty of protein directly from plant foods. Humans can obtain protein either directly by eating plants or indirectly by eating animals which have eaten plants. Obtaining protein through animals, however, involves a greater risk of contracting foodborne diseases, heart disease, and osteoporosis.

Planning a Healthy Diet

It is not difficult to plan a nutritionally complete diet from plant foods. Meticulous attention to food combining, weighing foods, calculating nutrients, and the like are things of the past. Instead, there are four simple guidelines to follow: (1) eat a variety of plant foods from each of the New Four Food Groups (vegetables, grains, fruits, and legumes); (2) make sure those nutrients formerly obtained from animal sources are included in sufficient portions (e.g., calcium, iron, protein); (3) eat enough calories to maintain a desirable weight and energy level; and (4) shift to whole grains and unrefined foods, since they contain more minerals and vitamins than refined foods.

Obtaining enough calories for energy is rarely a problem for vegetarians, because most of their calories come from carbohydrates. The term "calorie" is a measure of energy produced by food when it is metabolized in the body. The three primary sources of energy for the body are carbohydrates, fats, and protein. Nutritional experts recommend that about 70 to 80 percent of one's calories should be in carbohydrates, 10 to 15 percent of one's calories in protein, and 10 to15 percent of one's calories in fat. The typical America diet is about 37 percent fat. Carbohydrates, unlike fat and protein, are stored in muscle and liver tissue in a readily available form called glycogen. Glycogen is much like the gas in a gas tank; it is ready to supply energy whenever needed. Complex carbohydrates, such as rice, whole wheat, potatoes, and corn, provide long-term energy, whereas simple carbohydrates, such as refined sugar, provide only a short-term pick-up.

Complex carbohydrates fill us up and provide us with sufficient energy without causing us to gain weight. Contrary to popular opinion, carbohydrates are not fattening. It is the fatty substances we spread on our bread or put in our baked potatoes that are more likely to cause weight gain. Only when the body's glycogen capacity reaches its limit is it turned into fat. This, however, rarely occurs in an active person, since glycogen is continuously used for energy.

Many base their diet on the USDA food pyramid. The primary goal of the USDA, however, is to promote the interests of American agriculture (including the meat and dairy industries), not to protect the health of the American public. Neal Barnard advocates the New Four Food Groups as a healthy vegetarian alternative to the new USDA food pyramid (pp. 144–45). You will note that vegetable oils, nuts, and seeds are not on the following chart. They should be used sparingly due to their high fat content.

NEW FOUR FOOD GROUPS

Whole Grains   The whole grain group includes whole wheat bread, rice, millet, pasta, corn, and various whole grain cereals, such as oatmeal.

Vegetables	Vegetables comprise a large group that includes broccoli, kale, collards, cabbage, cauliflower, sweet potatoes, white potatoes, tomatoes, carrots, onions, garlic, lettuce, beets, peppers, squash, and much more.
Fruits	Fruits include apples, oranges, grapefruits, pears, peaches, apricots, plums, bananas, cherries, blackberries, blueberries, raspberries, strawberries, kiwis, grapes, figs, and melons.
Legumes	The legume group includes beans, lentils, peas, and tofu.

A vegetarian diet is not as drab as it might sound. Americans are accustomed to a slab of beef on their plate with a side dish of overcooked and unappetizing vegetables. No wonder so many are hesitant about adopting a vegetarian diet. Take away that meat and there is nothing really palatable left. However, in place of meat as the main course could be any number of delicious vegetarian entrées, such as tofu lasagna, bean burritos, vegetarian chili, heavenly stew, and the like. The side dishes of vegetables do not have to be overcooked and leached of all their vitamins, minerals, and flavor. Quick cooking in a pressure cooker produces delicious and healthy vegetables.

A gradual transition to vegetarianism is likely to be more permanent. It is very easy to become discouraged when attempting a sudden change, especially when you have not found good-tasting main dishes to take the place of the slab of meat. The best method is try one meatless main dish a week (such as those in this book) and increase the number as more are found that you like. At first you may want to try meat analogues (e.g., veggie burgers, soy hotdogs), but they are expensive and may contain high levels of sodium.

Closing Thoughts

It is advisable for those on medication or under doctor's care to check with their doctor before drastically altering their diet.

Special attention must also be given to growing children and pregnant and lactating women, who may need more calcium, protein, and iron. The information given above regarding nutrition and dietary guidelines merely summarizes recent research about the nutritional aspects of vegetarianism. It is not intended as medical advice, nor as a cure for any disease or condition. Medical advice and treatment of a disease or condition should be secured from a qualified medical professional. For documentation of the nutritional information included in the above discussions in a format accessible to lay persons, see *The McDougall Plan* or the more recent book by Neal Barnard, *Food for Life*. You can also check out the Tufts University Nutrition Navigator (http://navigator. tufts.edu/) for links to quality nutritional web sites.

Additional information can be obtained from various vegetarian societies and nonprofit organizations, such as The Vegetarian Resource Group, North American Vegetarian Society, EarthSave Foundation, and Physicians Committee for Responsible Medicine. Current addresses and data on these and other organizations can be obtained from the *Encyclopedia of Associations,* available at most libraries. Updated email and web addresses for these groups can be located through Internet search engines. The Vegetarian Resource Group web site (http://www.vrg.org) lists many vegetarian web sites and user groups.

Further
Reading

Adams, Carol J. *The Sexual Politics of Meat: A Feminist-Vegetarian Critical Theory.* New York: Continuum, 1990.

Barnard, Neal. *Food For Life: How the New Four Food Groups Can Save Your Life.* New York: Crown, 1993.

Berman, Louis A. *Vegetarianism and the Jewish Tradition.* New York: KTAV, 1982.

Bondi, Roberta. *To Love as God Loves: Conversations with the Early Church.* Fortress, 1987.

Charlesworth, James, ed. *Jesus and the Dead Sea Scrolls.* New York: Doubleday, 1992.

Fleming, Diana J., ed. *Country Life Vegetarian Cookbook.* Sunfield, MI: Family Health Publications, 1990.

Frei, Hans W. *The Eclipse of Biblical Narrative: A Study in Eighteenth and Nineteenth Century Hermeneutics.* New Haven: Yale University Press, 1974.

Hagler, Louise. *Tofu Cookery,* rev. ed. Summertown, TN: Book Publishing Company,1991.

Hauerwas, Stanley. *The Peaceable Kingdom: A Primer in Christian Ethics.* Notre Dame: University of Notre Dame Press, 1983.

Hays, Richard B. *The Moral Vision of the New Testament: A Contemporary Introduction to New Testament Ethics.* HarperSanFrancisco, 1996.

Johnson, Luke Timothy. *The Real Jesus: The Misguided Quest for the Historical Jesus and the Truth of the Traditional Gospels.* HarperSanFrancisco, 1996.

―――. *Scripture and Discernment: Decision Making in the Church.* Nashville: Abingdon, 1996.

Küng, Hans. *Eternal Life? Life After Death as a Medical, Philosophical, and Theological Problem,* trans. Edward Quinn. New York: Doubleday, 1985.

Lindbeck, George A. *The Nature of Doctrine: Religion and Theology in a Postliberal Age.* Philadelphia: Westminster, 1984.

Linzey, Andrew. *Animal Theology.* Urbana and Chicago: University of Illinois Press, 1995.

―――. *Christianity and the Rights of Animals.* New York: Crossroad, 1987.

Linzey, Andrew, and Tom Regan, eds. *Animals and Christianity: A Book of Readings.* New York: Crossroad, 1988.

MacIntyre, Alasdair. *After Virtue: A Study in Moral Theory,* 2nd ed. Notre Dame: University of Notre Dame Press, 1984.

McDaniel, Jay B. *Of God and Pelicans: A Theology of Reverence for Life.* Louisville: Westminster/John Knox, 1989.

McDougall, John A. *The McDougall Program: Twelve Days to Dynamic Health.* New York: Plume, 1990.

McDougall, John A., and Mary A. McDougall. *The McDougall Plan.* Clinton, NJ: New Win, 1983.

―――. *The New McDougall Cookbook.* New York: Plume, 1993.

Marcus, Erik. *Vegan: The New Ethics of Eating.* Ithaca, NY: McBooks Press, 1998.

Mason, Jim, and Peter Singer. *Animal Factories Update.* New York: Harmony, 1990.

Messina, Virginia, and Mark Messina. *The Vegetarian Way: Total Health for You and Your Family.* New York: Crown, 1996.

Moltmann, Jürgen. *Theology of Hope,* trans. James W. Leitch. Minneapolis: Fortress, 1991.

O'Donovan, Oliver. *Resurrection and Moral Order: An Outline for Evangelical Ethics,* 2nd ed. Grand Rapids: Eerdmans, 1994.

Pinches, Charles, and Jay B. McDaniel, eds. *Good News for Animals? Christian Approaches to Animal Well-Being.* Maryknoll, NY: Orbis, 1993.

Rachor, JoAnn. *Of These Ye May Freely Eat: A Vegetarian Cookbook.* Sunfield, MI: Family Health Publications, 1990.

Santmire, Paul H. *The Travail of Nature: The Ambiguous Ecological Promise of Christian Theology.* Philadelphia: Fortress, 1985.

Schwartz, Richard H. *Judaism and Vegetarianism,* 2nd ed. Marblehead, MA: Micah, 1988.

Singer, Peter. *Animal Liberation,* 2nd ed. New York: Random House, 1990.

Wasserman, Debra. *Simply Vegan: Quick Vegetarian Meals,* 2nd ed. Baltimore: Vegetarian Resource Group, 1995.

Wasserman, Debra, and Reed Mangels, eds. *Vegan Handbook: Over 200 Delicious Recipes, Meal Plans, and Vegetarian Resources for All Ages.* Baltimore: Vegetarian Resource Group, 1996.

Westermann, Claus. *Genesis 1–11: A Commentary,* trans. John J. Scullion. Minneapolis: Augsburg, 1984.

General Index

A

Abel, 67
Abelard, Peter, 74
Abraham, 54, 67
Accommodation, divine, 10, 12,
    31, 68–69, 72, 74
Acts of Thomas, 96
Adam and Eve
    clothed with animal skins,
        28–32
    diet after the fall, 32–33
    diet in the garden, 20
    reflecting divine image, 30
American Dietetic Association,
    168
Animals
    care of (in Torah), 84–85
    compassion toward (in church
        fathers), 90, 134, 135, 140
    covenants with (in Bible), 46,
        47, 83, 145–46, 156
    cruelty to, 44, 48, 82, 153
    devaluation of, 118–19
    for entertainment, 36
    ethical responsibility for, 24–25
    and experimentation, 34–35,
        143
    in food factories, 47–50, 143
    God's love for, 83–84
    Jewish attitudes toward, 81–83
    and rights, 37–38
    sacredness of, 58, 60–61, 62, 68
    and souls, 23–25, 83, 86, 137
    suffering of, 33, 41–42, 84–86,
        137
    trapping of, 36
    unnecessary killing of, 42, 44,
        70–71, 74, 110, 148–49,
        163–64
Animal Welfare Act, 35
Anselm, 74
Anthony, St., 132–33, 138
Aquinas, St. Thomas, xvii, 24, 57,
    82, 159
Aristotle, xvi, xvii, 24, 57, 82, 159
Asceticism, 3, 8, 118, 119–20, 130,
    132, 133
Athanasius, 132
Augustine, St., 136–38
Aulén, Gustaf, 74

B

Balaam, 85

Barnard, Neal, 108, 171, 175, 177
Barth, Karl, 53, 65
Basil the Great, St., 128, 133, 140
Berman, Louis, 44, 73
Beskow, Per, 6
Betz, Otto, 94
Bible, the
   and compassion to animals,
     83–86
   conflicting dietary motifs,
     xvi–xvii
   dietary practices condemned,
     124
   as inspired reflections, 22
   as narrative, xvii–xx, 50–51,
     61, 110–11, 147
   textual history of, 8
   and vegetarianism, 15–16,
     19–21, 95, 98–99, 120–21
Bondi, Roberta, 158
Brown, Peter, 137
Bruce, F. F., 123–24

C
Calcium, 108, 168, 170–72
Calories, 174–75
Calvin, John, xvii, 31
Campbell, T. Colin, 167, 169
Cancer, 34, 102–3, 105, 167
Carnivore problem, 21–23
Chickens, 42, 48–49, 106
Christian liberty, 122–24, 132,
    138, 162. *See also* Freedom
Church
   influenced by cultural norms,
     xvii, 91, 138, 159
   mission of, 119, 150
Church, views within the
   regarding community, 155
   regarding health, 103
   regarding salvation, 147
   regarding souls, 24
   regarding vegetarianism, xvi, 8
Chrysostom, St. John, 77, 128,
    133–34
Circus animals, 36–37

Clement of Alexandria, 70, 96,
    128–29
Clooney, Francis X., 163
Cockfighting, 36
Community, 16, 123, 148, 155,
    159–60
Cows, 48, 108
Creation
   devaluing of, 8, 115, 117–19,
     130. *See also* Gnostic
     dualism
   as good, 19, 118–19, 128, 131
   solidarity of, 144–45
Creation stories
   intent of, 21–23
   origin of, 16–18
   and vegetarianism, 18–21
Creutzfeld-Jacob disease, 106

D
Dairy industry, 48, 108
Damascus Document, 7, 95
Daniel (the prophet), 98–99, 121
Dead Sea Scrolls, 4, 7–8, 95
Death, 21, 143, 146, 148–49
Deontological ethics, xix, 85, 125,
    159. *See also* Ethics, types
Descartes, René, xvi, 82, 86
Deuteronomic tradition, 73
de Vaux, Roland, 70
Didache, 50
Dietary laws, 8, 78–83, 92, 99,
    121, 124, 131–32
Directional markers, xix, 62–63,
    84, 124–25, 154–57
Diseases of affluence, 105
Docetism, 2
Dominion, 19–20, 58, 61, 84
Dostoevsky, Fyodor, 15
Draize Eye-Irritancy test, 35

E
Ebionites, 93, 97, 119
Eden, visions of, 16, 18, 33, 56,
    58, 61, 141, 154

Elephants, 36
Elijah, 99
Enlightenment, the, 9, 91, 103, 159
Enuma Elish, 17
Epictetus, 104
Epiphanius, 92, 97
Eschatology, 18, 143, 144, 145, 149
Eskimos, xx, 58
Essenes, 4–5, 7–8, 93–95
Ethics
  decision making, 159–62
  of diet, xviii–xx, 161–64
  and narrative, xix, 147–48, 153–54
  types, xix, 38, 80, 124–25, 158–59
  See also Virtue ethics
Eusebius, 95
Evil, 66, 104, 142, 146–47. *See also* Gnostic dualism
Ewing, Upton Clary, 4–5, 7
Exodus, the, 16–18, 143

F
Fall story, 29–31
Fasting, 96, 98, 130, 136
Fish, xvi, 1–3, 5, 8–9, 12, 95, 129
Flood story
  food provisions, 44–45
  interpretation of, 46–47
  Noah's sacrifice, 45–46, 55
  pre-flood violence, 43–44
Foodborne diseases, 106–7, 174
Frahm, Anne, 102–3
Freedom, 10, 37, 53, 57, 62–63, 74, 75, 98, 112, 125, 154. *See also* Christian liberty
Fur industry, 28–29, 35–36, 143

G
Gilgamesh Epic, 44, 46
Gluttony, 98–99, 109–10, 128–29, 131, 133–36, 138, 162

Gnostic Christianity, 5, 96, 117
Gnostic dualism, 8, 97, 105, 117–18, 124, 128, 131, 138, 147, 156
God
  and animals, 83–84
  concedes meat eating, 10, 53–59, 61–63, 73
  as Creator, 17–18, 61, 143
  image of, 19, 25, 30, 156–57
  imitation of, 83–84, 156–57
  immutability of, 55–56
  incarnation of, 9–10, 12
  kingdom of, 42, 125, 144. *See also* Peaceable kingdom
  as liberator, 16–18, 143
  makes animal skin garments, 29–32
Gospel of the Ebionites, 3, 92–93
Gospel of the Holy Twelve, 4, 5–6

H
Hauerwas, Stanley, 145
Healing, 112–13, 156
Health
  as a Christian concern, 103–5
  and diet, 105–9, 167–68, 174–77
  in holistic perspective, 110–13
Health Research Extension Act, 35
Heart disease, 103, 105, 167, 174
Hegesippus, 95–96
Hicks, Edward, 140–41
Hippolytus, St., 130–31
Historical reconstructions, 3–4, 9, 90–92, 100
Holy Spirit, 99, 104, 105, 112, 147, 149, 157–58, 160
Hope, xviii, 12, 17–18, 21, 33, 112, 142, 143, 148–49, 154–55
Human anatomy and physiology, 22–23
Humane Society of the United States (HSUS), 36

I

Identity, 9, 16–18, 51, 87, 91, 99,
  113, 143, 163
Irenaeus, St., 30, 147
Iron, 172
Isaac the Syrian, St., 90

J

James (brother of Jesus), 95–96
Jeremias, Joachim, 2
Jerome, St., 128, 134–36, 138
Jesus
  and animal sacrifice, 71–72
  death of, 11–12, 73–74, 83,
    154
  diet of (biblical witness), 1–3
  and dietary laws, 11, 80
  as Essene, 4–7
  ethics of, xix, 1, 80, 87, 159
  as example, 11
  historical, the, 3–4, 7, 9, 90–91,
    100
  mission of, 11
  multiplication of fish and
    loaves, 3, 4, 5, 129
  as nonvegetarian, 9–13
  and the peaceable kingdom,
    144
  as vegetarian, 3–9
John the Baptist, 3, 92–95
Johnson, Luke Timothy, 11
Josephus, Flavius, 93, 94

K

Kaufmann, Yehezkel, 67
Kook, Abraham Isaac, 44, 73,
  155
Kosher/kosher laws, 77–78,
  81–83, 87
Küng, Hans, 142, 147

L

Lactovegetarians, xv
Ladd, George Eldon, 144

Lappé, Frances Moore, 173
Lethal Dose 50 Percent test,
  34–35
Lewis, C. S., 28
Liberation, 16–18, 46, 50, 146
Linzey, Andrew, 12, 37, 38
Lossky, Vladimir, 90

M

MacIntyre, Alasdair, 163
McDougall, John, xi, 108, 167,
  169–71, 174, 177
McFague, Sallie, xii
Mad cow disease, 106
Maimonides, Moses, 66, 74
Manichaeism, 97, 131, 134,
  136–38
Manna, 98–99
Manual of Discipline, 95
Marcionites, 130–31, 134
Matthew (the apostle), 96
Meat (animal flesh), biblical
    words for,
  Greek (*kreas*), 123
  Hebrew (*basar*), 99, 109
Meat (generic word for food in
    KJV), 2, 116–17
Meat eating
  demand for necessitating
    factory farming, 42, 123,
    162
  divine concession of, 10,
    53–59, 61–63, 73
  ethics of, 161–64
  and gluttony, 109–10
  and health, 105–7
  and sacrifices, 72–73
Milk, xi, 78, 84, 107–9, 167, 168,
  170–72. *See also* Dairy
  industry
Moltmann, Jürgen, xviii, 18, 19,
  142, 143, 148, 149
Monasticism, 127–28, 132, 133
Montanism, 130
Moral philosophy, xx, 148
Moses, 5, 54

N
Nephesh, 24–25, 58, 60, 85, 86
New Covenant, xix, 81, 158
New Four Food Groups, 174–76
Nicea, Council of, 8
Noachian Covenant, 46–47, 83
Noah, 41–47, 53, 55, 57, 59, 67
Noah's ark, 42, 44–47, 50, 140
Novatian, 131–32

O
Origen, 125, 127, 128, 131, 158
Ornish, Dean, 103
Osteoporosis, 103, 105, 108, 167, 171, 174
Ouseley, Gideon Jasper, 5
Ovo–lactovegetarians, xv
Ovovegetarian, xv

P
Paley, William, 53
Passions, 127–28, 131. *See also* Vices
Passover, the, 2, 65–66
Paul (the apostle)
  and dietary liberty, 122–24
  ethical method of, 121–22, 124–25
  and vegetarianism, 115–18, 120–22
Peace, xvii, 16, 18, 20, 141–42, 145–46, 156. *See also* Eden, visions of
Peaceable kingdom
  aspects of, 144–47
  and ethics, 147–48
  Isaiah's vision of, 141–42
  Jesus' preaching of, 144
  the painting, 140–41
  summary of, 150
People for the Ethical Treatment of Animals (PETA), 29
Pesticide residues in food, 106–7
Peter (the apostle), 96–97
Pigs, 49–50, 77, 78–79, 146

Plato, 24, 159
Plotinus, xvi
Plutarch, xvi
Porphyry, xvi
Priestly tradition, 18–19, 43–45, 55, 73
Protein, 168, 172–74
Pseudo-Clementine literature, 96–97
Pythagoras/Pythagoreans, xv, xvi, 115, 127, 129, 130, 131, 135

Q
Qumran community, 4, 7–8, 93–95

R
Rabbits, 35
Rad, Gerhard von, 61
Renewal, 155–56
Resurrection, 10, 12–13, 21, 83, 143, 148–49, 154–55
Revelation, 16, 18, 22, 31, 72, 74, 143

S
Sabbath, 85, 119, 130
Sacrifice, animal
  denouncement texts, 69–71, 161
  and Jesus, 71–72
  and Noah, 45–46, 55
  origins of, 67–69
Salmonella poisoning, 106, 108
Salvation, 21, 105, 112–13, 147
Samuel, 58–59, 69
Saul, 69
Schoeps, Hans-Joachim, 96, 97
Schwartz, Richard, 82, 107
Schweitzer, Albert, 1, 3–4, 41
Skriver, Carl Anders, 6, 7
Slaughterhouses, 41–42, 143, 146
Solomon, 85

Souls
  of animals, 23–25, 83, 86, 137
  of humans, 24
  transmigration of, 129, 131,
    135
Stewardship, 105, 109, 110
Suffering, 11–12, 84–85, 112, 149,
    154
Symbolic world, 54–55, 61–62,
    87, 107, 113, 120, 142
Symbols, biblical, 61, 154
  ark, 46–47, 50–51
  blood, 60–61, 68
  Eden, 16
  flood, 46
  cleansing creation of evil, 147
Szekely, Edmond, 5

T
Teleological ethics, xix. *See also*
    Ethics, types
Temple Scroll, 8
Tertullian, 115, 128, 129–30
Theissen, Gerd, 122
Thomas (the apostle), 96
Thoreau, Henry David, 171–72
Tillich, Paul, 145
Tolstoy, Leo, 41–42, 48
Total vegetarians, xv

V
Vaclavik, Charles, 4–5, 7

Veal calves, 48, 84, 108, 146
Veganism, xvi
Vegetarianism
  definition of, xv
  dietary planning, 167–68,
    174–76
  historical synopsis of, xvi
  public opinion polls, xv
  resources, 177
  types, xv–xvi
Vices, 74, 96, 99, 121, 123, 127,
    148–49, 150, 157, 159,
    161–62
Virtue ethics, xix, 38, 71, 80,
    121–22, 157–62
Virtues, 38, 87, 96, 99, 123, 128,
    138, 148, 157–61
Vitamin B_{12}, 168, 169–70
Vitamin D, 171
Vivisection, 28, 34–35

W
Weil, Simone, 85
Wesley, John, 102
Westermann, Claus, 22, 43,
    142
White, Ellen G., 59
Woolman, John, 153

Y
Yahwist tradition, 19, 29–31,
    43–45, 55

Recipe Index

Bread
Soybean Cornbread, 40

Breakfast
Granola, 126

Desserts
Carob-Coconut Frosting, 165
Carob Pudding, 113
Fudgy Brownies, 164
Granola Cookies/Bars, 151
Pumpkin Pie, 52

Main Dishes
Bean Burritos, 88
Broccoli Stroganoff, 13
Haystacks Unlimited, 75
Heavenly Stew, 151
Macaroni and "Cheese," 139

Meatless Loaf , 51
Millet Burgers, 100
No-Meat Balls, 76
Pasta Primavera, 113
Spanish Rice, 139
Taco Salad, 125
Tofu Lasagna, 26
Vegetable Rice Pilaf, 88
Vegetarian Chili, 39

Sauces and Spreads
"Cheese" Sauce, 27
Country-Style Gravy, 101
Hummus, 64
Sunflower Sour Cream,
13

Soup
Minestrone Soup, 63